WHAT IS RESEARCH?

Edited by PETER N. MILLER
Published by BARD GRADUATE CENTER

WHAT IS RESEARCH?

Series: BGC✕
Editor: PETER N. MILLER
Managing Editor: EMILY REILLY
Copy Editor: ANN-MARIE IMBORNONI
Art Direction and Design: EUROPIUM and JULIA NOVITCH
Cover Photography: EUROPIUM
Typeface: Common Serif by WEI HUANG

Published by BARD GRADUATE CENTER
Printed by PRINTON in Tallinn, Estonia
Distributed by UNIVERSITY OF CHICAGO PRESS

ISBN: 978-1-941792-24-7
Library of Congress Control Number: 2020943811

BARD GRADUATE CENTER
38 West 86th Street
New York, NY 10024
bgc.bard.edu

ABOUT THE PUBLICATION

BGC✕ publications are designed to extend the learning period around time-based programming so that it may continue after the events themselves have ended. Taking the spontaneous alchemy of conversation, performance, and hands-on engagement as their starting points, these experimental publishing projects provide space for continued reflection and research in a form that is particularly inclusive of artists.

This book is an edited record of the conversation series titled "What is Research?" that took place at Bard Graduate Center in New York during Fall 2019. The program gathered a group of artists, scientists, and humanists—all MacArthur Fellows—for three evenings of discussion, featuring Annie Dorsen, Elodie Ghedin, Tom Joyce, Hideo Mabuchi, Campbell McGrath, Peter N. Miller, An-My Lê, Sheila Nirenberg, Terry Plank, and Marina Rustow.

"What is Research?" was supported by an X-Grant from the John D. and Catherine T. MacArthur Foundation's Fellows Program. We are grateful to the foundation for its interest and support and, in particular, to Krista Pospisil for her care and attention to this project.

Special thanks to James Congregane, Kate Dewitt, Amy Estes, Leon Hoxey, Jocelyn Lau, Dan Lee, Kristen Owens, Hellyn Teng, and Maggie Walter.

Campbell McGrath
At the Ruins of Yankee Stadium

It is that week in April when all the lions start to shine,
café tables poised for selfies, windows squeegeed
and fenceposts freshly painted around Tompkins Square,
former haven of junkies and disgraceful pigeons

PETER N. MILLER: Bard Graduate Center (BGC), which is celebrating this year its 25th birthday, is a graduate research institute. We have MA and PhD programs; we have an exhibition gallery; we publish a monograph series, *Cultural Histories of the Material World*, and two journals, *West 86th* and *Source;* and create digital projects through our digital media lab. Research is the matrix that binds all these activities together and mutually informs them, and so research is something that we think about all the time.

Which brings us to the really astounding point that research is not something that the scholarly community thinks much about. In the global economy of knowledge, research is the thing that drives everything. The estimate is that over a trillion dollars is spent annually by governments, the private sector, and educational institutions on research. To take one easy, low-hanging piece of data, there are, as it turns out, about 164 million items in the Library of Congress' catalogue. But if you search under the subject heading "Research—History," you will find 43 items (or at least that was the number last night when I checked). Even if that subject listing is notoriously spotty, I think we can say that it's still a remarkably low number for a subject of such great importance.

Research is what we do; it's what we think about; it's how we evaluate ourselves. But nobody studies it or thinks about it as a thing. It's our cultural blind spot. And cultural blind spots, when you can find them, are *always* worth studying. The absence of attention, the taking of something for granted, can speak volumes about a society.

We are asking this question, "What is research?" precisely in order to light up this blind spot. We think it's important. And not just because it's what we do at BGC or because of the huge amount of money committed to R&D. Research is important because it's at the heart of the modern world. Almost everything associated with science, technology, and our human self-understanding has exploded in the last 150 to 200 years because of research. Forget about planets visited or nano-landscapes explored. Research has

today chock-full of French bulldogs and ornamental tulips

transformed how we go about thinking about thinking. If, in the past, that kind of cultural definition and self-definition was mediated through priests and backward-looking tradition, in the modern episteme we systematically march into the future armed with our one-tool-to-fit-all-problems: research. If everything points to research, I think there's an argument to be made that research also points back out to everything. Let me explain. Think about the kind of personal and intellectual virtues you need in order to do research. There's persistence, determination, imagination, organization, self-criticism, love of truth, collaboration, communication, and long-term vision. If we step out of the archive or the laboratory, we might see these same virtues as describing not the excellent researcher but the excellent human being—or at least one kind of excellent human being. Mapping the epistemic virtues associated with research—or in simpler terms, recovering the meaning of research for the researcher—also means uncovering a vision of human excellence. We could even see it as a political vision, since the idea of a democratic citizen—and this takes us back to Jefferson's notion of the importance of a training in the liberal arts in the new United States—requires many of these same skills in arguing, collaborating, and pursuing truth in a self-critical sort of way. (I'm not going to do more than underscore the question I've just posed, implicitly, about the relationship between research and the liberal arts, but it could be said to go to the heart of the broader question about the relationship between teaching and research that has vexed the university for the past 200 years.)

One more point about this portrait of research we are sketching: it's actually much more about question-asking than answer-giving. And this is where we have to bring in some history. The antiquarians of early modern Europe, who began the process of putting back together the Humpty Dumpty of the ancient world—and whose object- and text-handling methods were soon taken over by historians and then farmed out among the newly minted humanistic disciplines of the 19th century, such as art history, archeology, anthropology, and sociology—are acknowledged as the first

superimposed atop the old, familiar, unevictable dirt.

to do research on the past. They excavated, both in the dirt and in dusty archives. What they had was curiosity—and in spades. It was their mark, and it filled the *Kunst-* and *Wunderkammern* that have inspired contemporary artists from Joseph Cornell onwards.

As an aside—and I just can't resist—this was such an ingrained association, at least once upon a time, that when Marcel Proust wanted his readers to understand what a lover's passion really looks like, he described the desire to know every square inch of a lover's body with the antiquary's endless curiosity for, and I'm quoting, "the deciphering of texts, the weighing of evidence, and the interpretation of old monuments." Not necessarily the first comparison that might now come to mind, right? But Proust did signal in the very title of his book that what we think of as research could, on the individual level, be very close to the core of the human experience. (If *recherche* in French can also mean "search", *chercheur* means "researcher"—so the ambivalence should be seen as productive.)

But as much as this kind of curiosity may have led the antiquarians to do research, what we call research is not the same as curiosity. Curiosity is in it, but research is different. Curiosity in the researches of people like Nicolas Fabri de Peiresc (1580–1637), to take one example I happen to know well, went out in all directions. Modern research is focused by the question that it asks. The question helps draw a line between what we need to know and what might be nice to know, but which we don't need in order to answer our question.

War made the 20th century *the* century of research. The Second World War played a key role. Think about space research and everything that's spun off of it—all the civilian applications. That came right out of work on captured V-2 rockets begun immediately after the war and—it needs to be said—with captured Nazi scientists. But we've also lost something in this translation. In 1930, in Hamburg, two German scholars published a two-volume work that was a history of research institutes, along with short reports written by members of 65 institutes, along with 10 international surveys, in

Lying on the couch, I am drifting with the conversation

the humanities and sciences. In 1934, in Vienna, the young Karl Popper published a book on research in the sciences with the title *Der Logik der Forschung*. But in 1959, when the book came out in English, its readers—and given how important the book was, that's a big number—encountered a work with the title *The Logic of Scientific Discovery*! "Research" had disappeared. Thinking about research was fully now assimilated to thinking about scientific method. A scholarly generation later this process is so far along that research isn't even noticed when it's done by scientists. So, if you go to Latour's *Laboratory Life*, which is his deep ethnography of what goes on in a laboratory—it happens to be at the Salk Institute in La Jolla, maybe the most important research institute in the world from an architectural point of view—he never once turns his roving brain to the notion of research, even though he'll talk about the scientists there as researchers doing research. The whole book is an ethnography of the research process, but he never stops to ask about research. For him it's laboratory science that he sees in front of him. Not research. It's that blindspot again.

It is in this spirit of question-asking, then, that BGC kicks off an inquiry—which will end with an exhibition in our gallery in 2023—with a conversation. And who better to introduce us to the meaning of research than a group of people who are our culture's heroes of research? We've gathered nine MacArthur Fellows as our panelists for this discussion. They include artists, humanists, and scientists. We've brought them from these different backgrounds because at the beginning of our inquiry we're not going to presume that there is only one kind of research. We can't answer the question "What is research?" until we know more about the whole spectrum of research. Nuance really is the key. As Aby Warburg, one of BGC's patron-scholar saints once said, "The dear god is in the details." We might add to it today: "... in the conversation."

of bees, a guttural buzz undergirding the sound

I.

PETER N. MILLER: Let's begin by asking our panelists to say a few
 words about their own work as it relates to research. And
 then we'll start asking some questions.

AN-MY LÊ: I'm a photographer, and I have made work that's mostly
 drawn from my autobiography. I'm Vietnamese-American,
 and I came to the United States at the end of the Vietnam
 War in 1975 when I was 15. I first was trained as a biologist
 and had plans to go to medical school. I ended up working
 in a research lab, and did get into medical school. But then
 I discovered photography and made the switch, and my work
 is a little bit like a scientist, but also as an artist. It should
 be interesting to think about research in that way. I think
 that my work requires a lot of research, and I use the word
 research in a very broad way. It's about getting access.
  In the early '90s, Vietnamese-Americans were able
 to return to Vietnam when President Clinton renewed
 relations with Vietnam. So, I was able to go back to Vietnam
 and photograph there. The next project that I did had to do
 with the memory of the war, and being the photographer
 who likes to be there and photograph in the real world, the
 only thing I could find that would satisfy that question and
 that subject was to photograph Vietnam War re-enactors. I'd
 gain access to that group and work with them. And as I was
 finishing, we invaded Iraq, and I think this idea of the consequences of war—the idea of the effect of war—really was
 extremely distressing to me.
  I wanted to go to Iraq but was not able to become
 an embed, so I found a way to photograph the Marines
 who were training outside of Los Angeles. At Joshua Tree
 [National Park], I thought the landscape was really exciting
 and similar to Afghanistan. So, I went there and photographed them, and it turned out to be something interesting.
 Because you didn't have to deal with the devastation, and

you could actually think about war, and think about the preparation for war, and perhaps the consequences. And then I sort of switched and became interested in the military in real time—and what they were doing all over the world—and that required a lot of research and access. More recently, I started a project that is a kind of re-imagined American road trip that was prompted by an invitation I had to a period film—a Civil War filmset with battle scenes and trench wars. At the same time, Confederate monuments were being contested, and I just sort of pulled it all together. So, I've been working on this kind of American road trip and trying to take a pulse of the political and social aspects of our culture today.

TERRY PLANK: Wow, I don't have great pictures, so I'm just going to have to paint them in your mind's eye. I work on volcanoes. Everything from where the magma comes from, why some are more explosive than others... and right now I'm working on sulfur. So, how many people here have been to a volcano? And it smells, right, when you go? It's literally brimstone, so sulfur is an important part of what comes out of volcanoes. We think it's an important precursor that it is something you can measure from space remotely. But we don't really know where the sulfur comes from. Is it entrained in the magma? And then where did that come from?

The volcanoes I study are part of the plate tectonic cycle. They're the ones that are around the Pacific, the Ring of Fire, where the Pacific plate is subducting into the Earth. And it brings the sea floor with it—and sulfur ultimately with it. So, our hypothesis is that the sulfur is actually coming from seawater—from the ocean—and it gets subducted, and then is part of the melting process that makes magma and comes back to the surface. These kind of cycles are what I've been working on—not just the volcano, but its origins in the plate tectonic cycle.

In terms of research, I've been trying to think about how to categorize this in some way. Part of what we do is kind of frontier analytical measurements. There is one

in the overgrown beech tree marooned out back,

instrument in the UK right now that can measure sulfur isotopes—really tiny proportions. And there are only a few instruments that can XRF scan an entire deep-sea core where the sulfur is residing. The other part is actually going to volcanoes and measuring stuff. Earth science is fantastic because it's still such a young field. You know that plate tectonics was discovered here, in New York, at Columbia University, in the 1960s? We invented subduction with the plates sinking into the mantle. It's still a very young field, and we're still very data-limited, and so we still go in the earth and explore. I've been working in Alaska most recently with the active volcanoes in the Aleutian Islands. Three are erupting right now. You may not know about that, but if you happen to fly from North America to Asia—like 60,000 people a day—you fly over Alaska Volcano Airspace.

MARINA RUSTOW: So, I'm a historian, and I study a very particular cache of texts that were preserved in a medieval synagogue in Cairo—a synagogue that was built in the 11th century, and that had a storeroom for worn manuscripts. And over the course of the late 19th century, about 400,000 fragments came out of this synagogue and were distributed to libraries and private collections in lots of different places, primarily in Europe, but not only. And of this cache, about 40,000 fragments are what historians call "documentary texts"—meaning, texts that weren't meant for long posterity, such as letters, legal documents, grocery lists, literally tax receipts. Which sounds really boring, but, like, I have a crush on tax receipts right now. I find them totally fascinating—not so much like 21st century taxes, but the 11th century ones are fascinating to me.

     The languages that the texts I read are written in are, first of all, Arabic, but because most of the people writing these texts were Jews, they were writing Arabic in Hebrew characters. Which 20th century scholars called Judeo-Arabic, but people then would have just called it Arabic. They also wrote some Hebrew, and some Aramaic, which was used for

limbs shaggy with neon-green flame-tongue leaflets

very limited purposes by the 11th and 12th century. But I also read Arabic script documents.

I'm a social historian, which means that I like to understand history really from the ground up... people's daily lives. The first time I ever went to an archeological excavation and saw a medieval latrine was one of the happiest moments of my life, because I had not understood how people went to the bathroom in the 11th century before then. I'm studying a time and place from which there are very few continuously surviving archives—where almost all the documentation that we have has been preserved either accidentally or has been dug up archeologically. We're constantly faced, in my field, with this problem of lack of information.

An 11th- or 12th-century document from the Cairo Geniza, pieced together from three fragments. The text is a florid Arabic poem in praise of the competence of a government bureaucrat, copied in alternating lines by two state officials, probably master and disciple. Cambridge University Library, T-S Ar. 42.196 + T-S Ar. 30.316 + T-S Misc. 5.148. Reproduced by kind permission of the Syndics of Cambridge University Library.

HIDEO MABUCHI: My training is in physics—mainly atomic physics and optical physics—and for the past 20 years or so, I've run a research group that really focuses on foundational studies in quantum engineering. So, if you can imagine, we're kind of trying to refurbish some of the core theory and methodology of engineering to make it ready for what we're going

forking through a blanket of white blossoms,

to be doing with nanoscale systems in the coming decades. We do both a combination of experimental research—so mostly, in our labs, our laser labs—and we do quite a bit of theoretical and computational work, which has to do with trying to understand a little bit better how theories like quantum mechanics apply to real technology. In that part of what I do, like much academic physical sciences research, I'm really managing a research group of graduate students and sometimes postdoctoral scholars. So, I would say, in terms of my own engagement with it, it's a research manage-

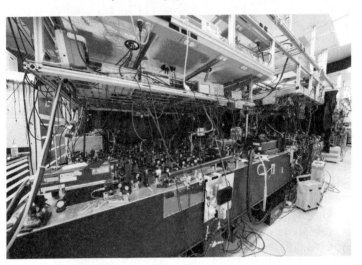

Apparatus that incorporates laser-cooled atoms and a nondegenerate optical parametric oscillator in a coherent feedback loop to demonstrate coherent wavelength-shifting of a nonlinear response function, of course! Courtesy of H. Mabuchi.

ment kind of thing, and then I'm working very hard to try to get money to support that research—which is what academic research in the sciences these days is largely about. It's very rare that I would say I get to really engage in a deep and meaningful way with something that's at the forefront of the kinds of things that my group's work is concerned with.

So, somewhat as a reaction to that, or maybe just because it was time, I have had this growing personal interest in studio ceramics. Mainly wood-fired vessels, wheel-thrown and altered. I put a lot of time and energy into that, as a maker of ceramics. I'm also very interested these days in talking

long-neglected evidence of spring at its most deluxe,

about ceramics, writing about ceramics, developing medium analysis and a kind of critical theory that applies to contemporary ceramics. But then I'm also, as a physical scientist, going into a traditional craft area where you dig clay out of the ground and stick it in a wood-burning kiln, and you see all these colors, textures, appearances, surfaces. And it's hard not to wonder what's going on there, in detail. It's where I do get to re-engage with the scientific part of my interests and abilities. I'm very interested in studying the physics and chemistry of the development of ceramic surfaces. For a while, it was a sideline where I felt like I was cheating on my day job, but I do these days focus very heavily on trying to integrate this aspect of what I do into the kinds of teaching that I do as an academic. I'm very interested in teaching that bridges the STEM fields with the humanities and with art practice.

SHEILA NIRENBERG: My research focuses on what's called "neural coding." What we work on is the general question of how the brain takes in information from the outside world and converts it into patterns of electrical pulses, and how we make meaning out of that. So, just as an example, you're looking at me right now and you see my face, and that gets represented in your brain as patterns of electrical pulses. And it's different from the patterns if you're looking at other people. So, at first glance, you think, "It's just like a photograph. I would clearly be able to distinguish it from a photograph." But what the brain does—and what the visual system does—is that it pulls out the parts of, let's say, my face that you need to know, so that if I left the room and came back, you could recognize me. It doesn't hold on to every freckle or every eyebrow hair, because you don't need to know it. It's a fascinating question: what is it actually holding on to, to allow us to recognize people? Partly, it doesn't do that good of a job, actually, and that's why people are really bad as witnesses in a crime scene. And we stereotype all over the place, which is also a whole fascinating side project.

pure exuberant fruitfulness run amok.

So, this is what I've generally been working on, and then, in the process, I cracked one of these codes: the code that goes from visual input from your photoreceptors to your optic nerve that sends signals up to the brain. And after I figured this out, it made me aware that I could make a prosthetic device for blind people. I could make a device that could mimic that transformation. I had this sudden awareness of it, and then the responsibility that went immediately

Bionic sight prosthetic. Courtesy of S. Nirenberg.

with that. So, I started a company, and then came all the things you have to do to actually bring something forward to patients. One has this idea as an academic that, you know, you're a scientist, and of course if you have an idea, grants will allow you to bring it to patients. But it doesn't work that way. It takes an enormous amount of money. So the best thing that I could do was patent it and then go to rich people and try to raise the money to do the idea, which is what I did. And just today I sent the last part I have to send to the FDA so that I get clearance.

So that's one half of what I do, and the other half is using this code as a front-end to computer vision. And to see if we can make robots parse information the same way that we do. We've done this with face recognition and self-driving cars and emotion detection: if we can see it, then the robot should be able to see it. All the little subtle things that we see in people's faces—like the difference between a real smile

Rigorous investigation has identified two dialects

and a snarky smile or a sarcastic smile—it's so fascinating to see how that's represented in patterns of neural activity. So I started a company on that one, too.

Ideas are just plain interesting, and I can't help myself. If I have an idea, I have to follow it. It's a beautiful part of life, in a way. So I'm not taking a great vacation and I'm not buying a plane. Not that I could ever afford to! But I don't care. The joy is figuring things out and making them useful to other people. Anyway, that's my story.

TOM JOYCE: As a sculptor, I have been forging iron for 49 years, and the initial impetus to work iron was founded in the small community where I grew up, in El Rito, New Mexico. But the more I understood about iron, the more it took me around the world with hammer in hand to understand things about other cultural groups that are also forging this material, this plentiful material. When one looks at the history of iron on the planet, you realize that our entire electromagnetic field is generated in a core of iron that's churning in dynamic movement to keep us in orbit around the Sun. And, at the same time, there is this availability of iron close to the Earth's mantle that is able to be mined to the tune of 1.5 billion metric tons a year. It was astonishing to me. And one of the initial aspects of thinking about iron in the world was looking at the symbiotic relationship that iron particles in the sea had with the very first life forms, cyanobacteria, that created oxygen as a by-product.

Fueled with that understanding of why iron is flowing through our bodies and this availability of material to be able to be worked, it meant that with everything that I forged, I felt I had to have some understanding of the deeper consequences of using this material. Each one of the ingots that I work with has, at the very top of it, all the impurities that settled on top of this molten pool of iron. Each one is different and as unique as the human fingerprint. So, the process that I go through in the work now is to find these very unique aspects of the material that you wouldn't

buzzing through the plunder-fall, hovering black bumblebees

be able to see otherwise. Once a piece has been forged, it looks homogenous; after machining, it looks pristine. But in going through an erosive process of heating that material to extreme temperatures and then cooling it very rapidly, I can expose the internal grain structure that has developed as a crystalline matrix in the sculptures that I'm working with. Just to give you a sense of the scale, some are three to four tons and go through a cycling process that can last up to two years, where it will be hundreds and hundreds of quenching cycles to be able to get that to happen. These are some of the strongest materials that metallurgists have ever conceived of—usually for military contracts—and what I'm trying to do is find the fragility in that material, to find the breaking point of materials that are not meant to break. My trajectory, I would say, is one

Aureole VI, forged stainless steel, 75" × 75" × 4", 4,407 lbs. Courtesy of T. Joyce.

and overworked honeybees neck deep in nectar-bliss,

that looks at the multiple uses of iron in our world at an industrial scale, where they are indispensable to our lives in the same way that blacksmiths were for thousands of years before the Industrial Revolution created the manufacturing wherewithal to make some of the largest forgings we've ever seen. Working in this factory outside of Chicago allows me to keep my finger on the pulse of what's happening inside that world that we're so dependent on, but it happens behind closed doors so we don't realize that the clothing we wear, the cars we drive, the planes we fly, would be absolutely impossible to manufacture were it not for blacksmiths working furtively around the clock on our behalf.

ANNIE DORSEN: I group a series of projects under a moniker that I made up in 2012 called "algorithmic theatre," and I started using that phrase because I was trying to distinguish what I'd started doing from multimedia performance—or from "robot" stuff. People started asking me, "How's it going with your robot theatre?" And I'd have to sort of say, "It's not robot theatre!" But what it was, was an attempt to think through how algorithms could be written that might generate theatre. I was influenced a lot by John Cage and the first generation of visual artists who called themselves "the algorists"—that's Roman Verostko, Mark Wilson, Manfred Mohr, in particular. But there was a whole generation from the late '60s and '70s who started doing "computer theatre" for the first time. I was really interested in the relationship between procedures and performance. In theatre, there's a whole set of assumptions that don't often get questioned about a kind of continuity—an idea of human nature that is continuous all the way back to the Greeks: that somehow it's the same eternal truths about human behavior that we recognize in Aristophanes or in Sophocles, and that track all the way through Shakespeare and Brecht to today. And I thought one way of maybe questioning that assumption was to work with computer programmers to write computer code that would produce theatre. What that actually has

as the city to us, blundering against its oversaturated anthers meant in practice is a piece called *Hello Hi There* that has two chatbots who generate a new dialog live in real time at every performance. The revenge of the machines!

They're talking about questions of language and creativity and human nature—all questions I was interested in—but of course they're quite digressive and don't really stay on topic very well. And then I made a piece called *A Piece of*

A scene from Annie Dorsen's *Hello Hi There*. Steirischer Herbst/W. Silveri.

Work, which was an adaptation of *Hamlet*, where I designed—again working with computer programmers—a series of algorithms that would kind of create in real time an adaptation of the play *Hamlet* at every performance, and would auto-generate the underscoring, the lighting, the scenic design, all the elements—almost like a literal "*Hamlet* machine." And, finally, *Yesterday Tomorrow* is the last in that series of proper algorithmic pieces that uses two pop songs, the song "Yesterday" from the Beatles and the song "Tomorrow" from the musical *Annie*. We designed an algorithm that would slowly change the notes and the syllables of the first song into the second song. I worked with three incredible contemporary music vocalists who would sight-sing the score as it was being generated. So,

until the pollen coats our skin, as if sugar-dusted,

it was a piece about metaphors of time, basically—about computational time, musical time, metaphoric time; about past, future, and how we fantasize about those things. That's been the work I've been mostly doing.

CAMPBELL MCGRATH: I write poetry—I'm a poet. The other kind of items that got listed on my CV are, like, accidents that I wandered into and I disclaim. I mean, I have a policy which I teach my students: just say yes before the person even finishes asking you to. "Hey would you be interested in our—" "I'll do it. Whatever it is. Let's go." So, you know, efforts I've done in theatrical or performance stuff, or more recently, working with poetry and visual artists—which I really enjoy doing. There's a lot of that happening in Miami. I always say yes but it's not something I claim any mastery of or knowledge of. I do it because I don't know what I'm doing, and it tends to help me enlarge what I do think I know how to do. Which is writing poetry, which I've been doing since I was a teenager, and just thought was a thing I liked doing. It slowly dawned on me that it was potentially, like, you could just keep doing it for your whole life, and you'd be 57 years old sitting on a stage, and you're still just doing the thing you liked doing when you were 16. It takes a combination of luck and skill and things falling a certain way, but that's basically the only thing I know, is how to write poems. I just keep doing it—I write. I've been doing it for so long that I write poems in a lot of different ways. Once you've written a book, and maybe a second book, you say, "What else might I do?" or, "How could I either enlarge or change or engage differently with the very notion of what poetry might be?" I mean, I published my 11th book this year, and I kind of like the notion that no two of them are the same—no two of them have quite repeated the same thinking about poetry or the same steps. Hopefully, they also still have a voice that people might recognize, but not also somehow feel like, "Well, he does that one thing over and over again."

Over time, I've come to realize that I probably

as if rolled in honey and flour to bake a cake

should have been a documentary filmmaker or something instead, because I really, really enjoy poetry as a documentary medium, which is not a common way to think of poetry. And so, of my 11 books, more or less every other one is a kind of historical-documentary project that takes on some aspect of the world. My third book, *Spring Comes to Chicago*, is really mostly a long poem called "The Bob Hope Poem," which is a kind of giant intellectual exploration of Bob Hope. But it turns out, really, Bob Hope is kind of a predecessor of the whole notion of the "cultural-military complex" that has projected American culture around the world in a very strange way. All these other thoughts grew out of that. I wrote a poem called "The Florida Poem" twenty-five years ago; it's like going to Mars to actually move to South Florida from Chicago. So that book explores—historically and kind of biologically—the world of Florida, the history of Florida, which has always been buried. Most recently I wrote a book called *XX: Poems for the Twentieth Century*. Again, a kind of historical project where I imagined: "Can you tell the story of the 20th century in poems written in personae—written in the voices of historical characters?" It's a hundred-poem-long sequence—one for every year of the 20th century—written in the voice of a character that had some significance to that year. In the intervals between those grander projects, I just write regular old lyric poems of various sorts. But I do like pushing poetry towards its intellectual and physical boundaries on the page. So, that's what I do.

ELODIE GHEDIN: How can I beat that? Alright, so as to my training, I'm a parasitologist—not a parapsychologist as some may think. I like bugs, OK? I've always liked bugs, but what I do is I decode the genomes of these bugs, and I'm pretty agnostic on what I'll decode. So, as long as it has genes, I'll try to figure out what they are.

I work on viruses, parasites, bacteria. In my field, people tend to focus a lot, so they'll be an expert in "x" and/ or "y." I've had trouble doing that. My expertise has been

for the queen, yes, she is with us, it is spring and this

using computational tools—using molecular tools—and then trying to apply them to various things. So, I started out working on neglected tropical diseases—diseases that affect what we call the "bottom billion," or regions of the world where they can have virus infections, bacterial infections, worm infections. I'm interested in how these microbes and parasites and all of these pathogens interact with their host.

These are pictures of the parasitic worms I work on. *Brugia malayi* (parasitic worm) with *Caenorhabditis elegans* (non-parasitic worm). Courtesy of E. Ghedin.

One aspect we've been working on is the fact that, in some parts of the world, people are exposed to so many microbes that they don't have certain diseases that we have in this part of the world—for example, some allergies, autoimmune diseases like multiple sclerosis, Type 1 diabetes. The occurrence of these diseases is much lower in some parts of the world where people are more exposed to microbes, because there's a co-evolution of microbes and of the host throughout the evolution of our species. And so what we try to do is understand how microbes are interacting with their host, and even to identify some molecules that these pathogens are secreting out that could maybe be used as or isolated as therapies. That's one aspect of my research. I also work a lot on flu—trying to predict what new strains are emerging every season—and on developing what would be a universal flu vaccine, where you don't have to worry about what strain is circulating every season. In a nutshell, what I do is explore what we call "host-pathogen interactions" using computational and genomic tools.

is her coronation, blossoming pear and crab-apple

II.

PETER N. MILLER: Great, thank you. Just to stay with you, Elodie, can you start us on the first question for the panel? How you do research as a scientist?

ELODIE GHEDIN: There are two aspects to it: there's a technical aspect and there's an intuitive aspect to research. And so when you train as a scientist, you train to learn what's called the "scientific method," which is basically the research method. The scientific method states that what you have to come up with first is a good question that is addressing a specific problem, and then there's a very technical and systematic way to try to answer that question by having a hypothesis. Hypotheses are actually not that easy to generate. You have to think in a very twisted way about what you think the answer is, and then your goal is to try to disprove the statement you've made. I think the easiest example is, you know, "Why is the sky blue?" It's like, "Ooh, observation: why is the sky blue?" And then the technical aspect is to say, "The hypothesis is that the light will go through gases in the atmosphere and will reflect off of the molecules, and it turns out that the blue light reflects more than the yellow and orange light, which goes straight. The blue light reflects, and it makes the whole sky look blue. My hypothesis is that the blue light is refracted by the molecules of the gases in the atmosphere." That's a hypothesis. And now I have to disprove it in my method. Now, research is never done in a vacuum, so when you say, "What's your method?," it's that I know there are gases in the air, but that means I've built my question or my hypothesis on knowledge that others have come up with. So, although it takes some type of intuition to come up with the question, you do have to base it on previous knowledge. What research should do—an aspect of the research—is to fold what you know of the past so that you can try to predict the future. And then, in predicting the

and cherry trees, too many pinks to properly absorb,

future, you try to refute that future with what would be the truth.

PETER N MILLER: Okay, thanks. Sheila?

SHEILA NIRENBERG: Well, you know, it's really testing a hypothesis. You have a thought, and you wonder if it's true. And then you lay out a way to test whether it's true or not true—but in a way that will allow you to distinguish between the gray areas. You want it to be a clean answer, so it's not giving you some hand-wringing thing that isn't satisfying.

PETER N. MILLER: Terry, how do you do research?

TERRY PLANK: Well, as I suggested, I think in our field it's a raw and young science that still has this chasm of ignorance. We are still so data-limited, so most volcanoes actually don't have functioning instruments on them. If there are instruments, most volcanoes don't have instruments that are telemetering or signaling data in real time. It's a huge wonderful opportunity, if we have a way to create arrays of instruments that can function autonomously, and speak to satellites in real time. We know volcanoes have a lot of precursors. We just don't measure them, and so there is just a raw discovery aspect to what we do.

Again, I have some colleagues from where I work up at the Lamont-Doherty Earth Observatory. And the discovery of plate tectonics that happened there was literally born from steaming across the sea back and forth, back and forth. They didn't even know what they were going to find. Every day they were setting off explosions, looking at the structure of the sea floor, taking a core, dragging a magnetometer. And, going back and forth they discovered, "Oh my goodness, there is a ridge in the middle of the ocean." We have adventures in

every inch of every branch lusting after beauty.

our science that are born from raw discovery, and data that no one else has even looked at before. And that's kind of my favorite thing to do.

MARINA RUSTOW: I think, rather than defining it, what I'd like to do is say what it is I do when I do research, which is read. Actually, I stare at really bad handwriting and generally feel inadequate. "If I were a better philologist, I'd actually be able to read this thing kind of thing." And so, I think it wasn't until I started to teach larger numbers of graduate students that I understood that there is actually no shame in not being able to read the stuff. I had been trained by a generation of people who thought that, you know, if your Hebrew or Arabic isn't perfect enough that you can just read something at a glance, then there is something fundamentally wrong with you.

Then you try reading an Arabic tax receipt where the scribe is not lifting the pen from the page for any reason whatsoever. And you can see that they're writing for other tax collectors. They're not writing to be read; they're writing in a secret code. And it's precisely that code that on the one hand is alluring because you want to crack it, and on the other hand, it's not meant to be cracked. There is a lot of it that's a battle royal with the texts. What I tell my students is that there is a "rule" that, like, 20% of your time will go into getting 80% of the job done. And then in that last 20% of reading the document, there are always those, like, five words that you can't decipher. And that's when you start Skyping with your colleagues all over the world. And if they can't read it, on the one hand, you're really happy because you feel less ignorant, and on the other hand, you're really sad because nobody is going to be able to read this thing.

It's really just a lot of very unromantic sweat and dictionary work. And then the question is, once you've done all of that sweat, can you make something beautiful out of it? I mean not so different from what you were saying—which is to say, can you think of a problem worth solving, and then write a narrative that somebody might actually want to read and know about once you're finished with all the sweat?

To this riot of stimuli, this vernal bombardment

What drives curiosity is lack of information. I have a historian guru named Carlo Ginzburg, an early modern historian who talks about the "euphoria of ignorance." It's this feeling that he experiences when he's about to embark on a new project about which he knows absolutely nothing. On the one hand, lack of information, on the other, the euphoria of ignorance. But then there is a third factor here, which is—and this is what fascinates me the most about the research process—false knowledge.

I'll give you an example: I've spent the last decade trying to understand why people petitioned the government in 11th and 12th century Egypt. And they would petition the government for incredibly mundane things. A true story: "My neighbor's son keeps biting my wife." Why would the sultan of Egypt care about this? The caliphs and sultans of Egypt would hear petitions about pretty much anything. When I started working on petitioning, I was really fascinated by the links between everyday subjects and government. There were two paragraphs in previous scholarship about how the petition and response procedure worked on a mundane level: like, who wrote the petitions, where you would bring them, and how they were processed. I thought two paragraphs was enough. I was like, "Great, this is an explanation of the petition and response procedure." And then I started digging into it and realized we know absolutely nothing about the petition and response procedure. And then I wrote 500 pages about it.

So, that process where a kind of gaping chasm just opens before you—and you thought you knew something and it turns out that you didn't—is the most exciting and fascinating part of the research process.

HIDEO MABUCHI: I guess I'm going to kind of draw a circle around all of that. Research is different things in different contexts. People will tend to think about research as a kind of problem-solving, which sometimes it is. But sometimes it's something completely different. I mean, I think just noticing stuff is a

of the senses, I have capitulated without a fight.

very important aspect of research. And, yes, especially in the sciences, there's a great component of hypothesis-driven research. But then I also feel that a lot of the most important research for the stuff that I really like to do just has to do with re-organizing the things that we think we already know. Research is searching, and when you're comfortable, you're kind of stuck in this little rut, and often what you really need is something to kick you out of that. Some discomforting thing, or some funny little thing that you notice that helps get you out of that local cul-de-sac. All of these different things are modes or aspects of research, and they apply depending on what you're doing.

PETER N. MILLER: If I can follow up with an interruption and ask you, Hideo, does "Hideo, the professor of physics" think about research in a different way than "Hideo, the artist?"

HIDEO MABUCHI: You know, I think as I've started to spend more time on things like ceramics and reading... I've come to realize that, I don't think I've ever really been a scientist... [*laughing*]. I've always been a bit of a frustrated artist who just happened to get a start working in the natural sciences. But, yes, I teach a course these days on creative process. It's a combined ceramics and physics thing. I have students working in the ceramics studio, in which I try to get them to experiment with a certain approach to creative process. And then I try to demonstrate for them how that same kind of approach can actually transfer into scholarly research, even scientific research. It follows a great book by William Kentridge, the South African artist, called *Six Drawing Lessons*. What he talks about in this book is what the creative process can be: you fill your mind with all the things that you're really interested in, and then you go to the studio and you just make up a bunch of games and play them for yourself. And then every once in a while you will notice something that just happens to pop out, that feels like it's related to something that you're

But not the beech tree. It never falters. It is stalwart

interested in, and you kind of follow that. And you can do that as a scientist, especially. Working in the physical sciences, which are an old scientific field, we have enough command of the basic materials and concepts that you can do that. But you can just screw around a little bit, or encourage your students to screw around. And I feel like the real creative work that I do as the professor is to notice when something interesting is happening—to try and relate different things that are happening, what the different students in my group are doing. I was really struck when I started reading things that artists have written about creative process. It really felt to me like the way I try to do scientific research.

PETER N. MILLER: Campbell, how do you do research?

CAMPBELL MCGRATH: I do write these kind of historical or investigative project books that, while on the page I want them to be poetry, intellectually I want them to be research projects. Like, I needed to know everything about the building of Chicago and industrialization to work on a section of "The Bob Hope Poem." Or, for that 20th-century book, I need to figure out, you know, modernism. I know what that is, kind of, because I saw some Picasso paintings. But what is it? What's the intellectual history and how would I then express it? It used to be that you went to the university library, but instead, now you go on Amazon and buy used copies of 27 books about it, and you just start piling up biographies and history books and aesthetic investigations and you start learning about it. On the other hand, when I write other books, you know, love poems or sonnets or whatever, that's just intuitive. That's like, "Oh, this little piece of language lodged in my brain." Or this thought, "I'd like to get that into a poem." And that's a purely, kind of, artistic method.

　　　I think of my main research method as something Walt Whitman says at the beginning of "Song of Myself," which is, "I loaf and invite my soul." Very famous line from

and grounded and garlanded, a site-specific creation,

near the beginning. "I loaf and invite my soul." Loafing around is my primary research method. I remember people always saying, "Campbell's just loafing around all the time. His life is not very difficult." Like, "No! This is research, man. I'm working." Right now I'm writing a book about the Atlantic Ocean and I live in Miami Beach, so basically every hour I spend staring at the ocean or swimming in it is research time, according to my doctrine. But it's actually true, that I'm deeply experiencing the thing I'm trying to write about and it isn't not being scientific. You know, it's intuitive. One day, you suddenly say, "Oh, I see. *This* is *that*. That's how I'm gonna write it. That's what I'm gonna say about the ocean." Or, "That's what I'm gonna think about this aspect of it."

As one final thought, there's a third aspect that is very true for me. It's that being in a physical landscape is very important to writing it. So even in the course of that 20th-century book, a lot of that research was about piling up biographies and stuff, but I also felt a need to go to the physical place, like Hiroshima or Auschwitz. Or if I was writing about Walter Benjamin, to explore his territories. And, you know, I can't say how that necessarily changed what I might have said about the history of that place or the voice that was speaking it, but it felt very important to me, and it still is a major source of inspiration for me. Physical landscape, being in a physical place in the world, often just starts a little train going that suddenly, at the end of the day—it may take a long time—becomes a poem.

PETER N. MILLER: Annie, where do you sit between the method in the lab and the loafing by the beach?

ANNIE DORSEN: I would like to be loafing. I'm quite familiar with the loafing method of research. But, you know, in my world, this question about research is interesting. This has been a hot topic in contemporary performance—in dance, and in theatre—and in visual art for about 20 years or so. But the

seed to rootling to this companionable giant,

idea that somehow there's such a thing as "artistic research," which is more like the scientific method than researching a topic that you're gonna write about—I don't know if I believe it, to be honest. The theory goes like this: practice is a form of knowledge acquisition and concept creation, and so the more you do, you try to design questions that you're going to try to answer, and you try maybe even to devise a hypothesis that you're going to somehow test through your artistic practice. Manfred Mohr wrote an essay in the early '70s about his process of making computer art that he was going try to teach a computer how to make images similar to the ones he'd been doing by hand. And I thought, "Oh, that's a great question for me to ask. How could I teach a computer how to make theatre?" And I sort of thought it was impossible. So, in a way it's even sort of learning by the negative.

And then I went ahead and tried to devise a method that would allow me to test whether you can teach a computer how to make theatre. First of all, what is theatre? What are the steps? What do people do when they get together to make theatre? Are we talking about a play? Are we talking about production? Are we talking about acting? So, you try to break it down into parts and figure out ways of attacking the problem. All that sounds good. It's a tricky question whether you're building on past research, whether you're leaving behind anything for others to do, and whether there is such a thing as being able to actually prove or disprove your hypothesis. That's where you get into tricky and subjective values and all this kind of stuff. In a way, you could say that I have a methodology that I've adopted from Cage or from Manfred Mohr—from any of these people—so it is somehow similar: there's something that they discovered, that I now go further with. And maybe in my work of adapting those techniques to theatre, I leave something for others to pick up and do. So, there is a lineage, but I'm not sure if it's quite the same animal.

ELODIE GHEDIN: Sounds the same.

tolerant and benign, how many times have I reflected

ANNIE DORSEN: Is it?

ELODIE GHEDIN: Yeah. It sounds completely the same.

ANNIE DORSEN: Really?

ELODIE GHEDIN: Yeah, yeah, yeah.

ANNIE DORSEN: That's interesting. I was all set to be kind of a naysayer. I mean, it got very trendy for a while—this notion that everyone's doing artistic research, and they're inventing new methodologies and techniques, and it all sounds super cool. But I always thought it was a bit of a fetish, because it's standing in for the rigor that we as artists are not sure that we have. You know, it's helping us feel that what we're doing is serious or something.

ELODIE GHEDIN: Right. But it is serious. I mean, it is—you are...

ANNIE DORSEN: Yes, but you know we always have this, kind of, low self-esteem about it—

ELODIE GHEDIN: [*laughing*] I love it.

ANNIE DORSEN: —compared to scientists, you know, the "real thinkers."

CAMPBELL MCGRATH: But the point is that, in science, the provability is the good work created through these methods, right?

upon their superiority to our species, the trees of earth?

It's kind of like, "Wow, the new methodologies!" But the methodology itself isn't what's important. It's the work that that methodology would produce, right?

ANNIE DORSEN: Well, you would think so. Because when it got kind of trendy, I remember sitting through, like, how many dance performances in the early 2000s, of people doing "dance research?" And these things were pretty unwatchable. I mean, they were doing something—and it was clear that they were all doing something—but what they were doing, I don't know. And then you have what is being communicated, and that is maybe where the analogy breaks down—where that encounter with a public, or with someone who is not in your field as part of your research team, or something: how do you communicate your findings?

ELODIE GHEDIN: Same thing.

ANNIE DORSEN: Yeah?

ELODIE GHEDIN: Same thing. How do you communicate? You understand in a very specific way, and then you have to relate that to people who are in your field. But, in general, when you write, you're writing for a very broad audience of scientists, and that's not easy.

ANNIE DORSEN: Yes.

PETER N. MILLER: Tom, how do you think about research?

TOM JOYCE: Yeah. You know, it's so funny, that question, really,

Reflection, self-reflection—my job is to polish the mirror, because I know that research is happening when I feel such a discomfort that I'm squirming in my seat about what it is that I think that I know. For me, research is generally working in the shadows, in the margins of what it is that I can anchor myself to, and a practice inside. Deep knowledge. It's moving outside of that comfort zone to be able to investigate things that are outside the area of expertise.

PETER N. MILLER: An-My, you mentioned having once been a research scientist. Does any of that stay with you in your work as a photographer?

AN-MY LÊ: I mean, I think one of the reasons why I became an artist is that I always felt that biology was just too narrow for me. And it never really allowed you to take a turn and then continue. You had to have a goal and stay within that goal. And as an artist, I feel that if you are inspired by something, you can just go ahead and do the research. And, maybe, your project will take a right turn and that would be OK. I mean, I suppose that there are some great scientists who discovered great things by taking that traditional turn, but it just seemed to me that you're not allowed to be so flexible. I think that there is also this issue of life, and I think life is so interesting. I wanted to be able to research life, and as a biologist I felt very constrained.

But what's interesting in terms of research is, as a scientist, when you talk about research, research is the work. And for a visual artist—even though it's changed—research is what you do to get you to make the work. I think there are a number of artists, especially activists now, who use the research as the actual work and show, for instance, this idea of archives. This idea of trying to gain access, and whether you can get it or not, you know—that's become part of the work and it shows the effort. For me, the research is everything that you do to help you get to the final result, which are the photographs for me.

to amplify the echoes. Even now I am hard at work,

TERRY PLANK: So, it's what you do ahead of time?

AN-MY LÊ: Yeah, and it starts with the hustling. What do you want to photograph? So, choosing your subject matter, and looking and seeing what has been done before. Is there something else for you to do? How do you get into a submarine? Or how do you photograph a volcano? Which scientist is going to help you get there? It's all that work, and it's very interesting, but I don't think that that work by itself will really change the quality of the final object. So sometimes people say, "Oh, you know, all that access—it's amazing." And it makes me look hard, because I think, "Well, OK, I got on the submarine. But is the picture really good?" So, it doesn't matter that I got on a nuclear submarine that went near the North Pole. The question is, "Was I able to make a great picture with that access?" It's always something that kind of tears me apart.

An-My,
Allow me to ask you some of the following questions to better assist you:

- How do you plan to meet the mission in Vietnam?
- Have you been cleared by the Vietnamese government?
- Are you dealing with anyone at the U.S. embassy in Vietnam?
- How long will you be staying?
- Have you received the U.S. Navy's Chief of Information's (CHINFO) approval through the Navy Information Office in New York City (NAVINFOEAST) who deal with book approval?
- Where do you plan on staying while in Vietnam?
- Have you previously worked with the U.S. Navy or any other element of the U.S. forces?
- Have you coordinated with the various NGOs/IGOs for approval should your book feature them in action?
- What requirements do you foresee needing either from, or a combination of, the U.S. Navy, USNS Mercy, and anyone else you can think of?
- Will you need to visit the ship at any point? If so, are you asking to spend nights onboard Mercy?
- If Vietnam doesn't materialize for you, what other country would you be interested in? The mission will be visiting Cambodia, Indonesia, Timor-Leste, Palau and Papua New Guinea.
- Finally, please add anything I may be overlooking.

I realize I've just presented you with a more questions than answers. However, I feel it will ultimately serve you best if I can prepare myself to speak intelligently about your project and goals.
V/r,

researching the ineffable. I loafe and invite my soul,

Pacific Partnership 2010 Public Affairs

███████

250 Makalapa Drive, Building 81
Pearl Harbor, HI 96860-3131
DSN ███████
Comm ███
Fax ███ █████████

Web: www.cpf.navy.mil

From: an-my [███████████████████████]
Sent: Thursday, January 14, 2010 7:49
To: █████████████████████████████
Subject: Re: Photography (U)

Dear ███████,
I would be available in the Spring and all summer as well. I am mostly
interested in the port visits in South East Asia in and around Vietnam.
Do you have a schedule yet?
Thank you so much for your help.
An-My

> On Jan 8, 2010, at 9:28 PM, ██████████████████████████████████
> wrote:
>
> An-My,
> As far as anything available this month I'm afraid to inform you
> that Pacific Partnership will not be able to assist you. We don't deploy
> until the Spring. Please don't hesitate to inform us of any additional
> openings in your schedule as they may arise.
> Cheers,
> ███████
>
> ███████████████
> Pacific Partnership 2010 Public Affairs
>
> ███████
> 250 Makalapa Drive, Building 81
> Pearl Harbor, HI 96860-3131
> DSN ███
> Comm ███
> Fax ███ ████████
>
> Web: www.cpf.navy.mil
>
> From: ███████████████████████████
> Sent: Friday, January 08, 2010 14:38
> To: an-my;
> Cc: ████████████████████████████████
>
> Subject: RE: Photography (U)
>
> I've copied ██████████████ (phone ████████) -- he is the
> ████████ for the this year's Pacific Partnership mission on
> the hospital ship USNS Mercy -- he can tell if you when there might
> be a good time to embark during their deployment.

for Walt Whitman is ever my companion in New York,

Phone:
Mobile:

From:
[mailto:]
Sent: Saturday, January 09, 2010 1:54 AM
To: an-my;
Cc:
Subject: RE: Photography (U)

Classification: UNCLASSIFIED

An-My,
Can you pls resend me a copy of your resume and the scope of
your current project that you want assistance with. We have a USNS ship
going through the Canal (APRIL) that I feel would be a good fit for
your request -

Thanks much

From: an-my
Sent: Monday, November 30, 2009 11:28
To:

Cc:
Subject: Photography

Dear   and   ,

I am following up on my request for support for my photography book
project.
I teach college photography and have a restricted travel schedule.
Our winter break is coming up so I would really like to take advantage
of that time to continue this project. I would really appreciate your
letting me know of any opportunities you may have from January 9th
to January 24th.

I am interested in photographing any cooperative activities our Navy
conducts in Asia and Central/South America such as actual operations
or even training that would involve Asian/South American militaries.
I am also interested in humanitarian/civil actions involving civilians.

For   : any locations: Caribbean, Central or South America
and of course a PANAMA CANAL CROSSING.
For   : any locations. I am also interested in a Navy hospital
ship operating in Vietnam.

I am grateful for your help. Please let me know if there is any
information I could provide or anything I can do to help expedite this
request.

All the best,
An-My

III.

PETER N. MILLER: Well, is the discussion right now about communication? Is that suggesting that research is somehow not for
the public? That research happens on this side of production,
but the outward-facing is not where you show your research?
That's one question.

        The other way of asking the question, I think, is
something that lurked in Annie's comment about lack of
rigor being troubling. I think it was played upon by Campbell
in the "loafing" comment. And that is: in Robert Caro's new
book called *Working*, he talks about his first editor at a small
local newspaper in New Jersey whose only advice to the
young investigative reporter was, "Turn every page." Right?
Research is about a certain kind of rigor more than anything
else. And so, the public-facing is the art, while research is the
rigorous, boring, churned-out, inward-facing activity. Is that
the dialectic that's at work here?

ELODIE GHEDIN: Well, I can comment on that. What's interesting
is that you can have good scientists and bad scientists, and
they may look the same on the "rigor" side of things, and it's
at the outward-facing that they may be very different. But
even then they may be very different in the question they've
asked. So, with a colleague of mine, we've been organizing
every month these things with drinks—you know, very re-
laxed, with colleagues. We call it "night science." Our prem-
ise is that "night science" is not hypothesis-driven, because
hypotheses often force you to look at where you think you're
supposed to be looking rather than just trying to find. And
so "night science" is where you have no hypothesis. I think
that will fit more with theatre, maybe, or art, or poetry. And
we do some loafing around as scientists, too. At night, that's
where ideas can come to you.

        It's the same thing in science where there are
certain intuitions that you have, and a lot of what I do is

and yet never un-nagged-at by loneliness, a hunger

just discovery. We'll do something just to see what happens, you know? Which is really hard to get funded. You'll write a grant, and you'll say, "I'm doing a fishing expedition." Going fishing is great. You find things that you're not seeking. You're really finding things. I think, as a scientist, that's important, too. But often you have scientists who will only seek. They're looking for a particular answer. I've had PhD students who will come to me crying and saying, "Oh, look at my results. It's not at all what I thought it would be." And then we'll look. I say, "Don't you see? It's much more interesting than what you thought it would be." And I assume that happens in what you guys do also. More in artistic endeavors where it can take you to places that you don't predict, right?

CAMPBELL MCGRATH: Absolutely, of course. I think in art if you really know the end result when you go in, it's almost guaranteed to be less interesting. The act of discovery for the artist tends to make the work exciting for the recipient, viewer, reader, whoever. You need to be exploring. Some things come off like, "Oh, that kind of actually went the way I thought it was going to go. What a surprise." But you need to be open to accept all those strange new turns, left turns, changes in the process. The process reveals everything in art. So, you start in with a great blueprint, and after that, a hypothesis, and, like, two lines in, the poem just says to you, "No, I'm totally not interested in that." And it takes a very long time to learn that you have to listen to the poem—that the poem knows more than you do—and it's a very dense, very counterintuitive thought. And students, it takes them forever to believe that they're not the master, that somehow the work is. Though you're the master of the work, it's a strange truth. But I do think, in terms of outward-facing and inward-facing, in general I believe all the hard work you put into the poem is to make it appear effortless to the reader. So, when students read Shakespeare's sonnets, they're like, "Well, that's easy. You can just do that, obviously." Like, "Look how easy it was for him? Just rolls off the old tongue there."

as much for the otherness of others as for the much-sung self,

Yeah, but that's the mastery of the craft. You can't do it, and I can't do it. He could do it, and so you read it and you're like, "Ah, he could have written another 150 of them." But that's an aesthetic issue, because then there are people that say, "Oh, all art is beautiful on the surface, and we need to roughen it up and destroy that notion of beauty and go in some other direction." But even in those works, the work of creating the work goes into making it look to the observer, reader, viewer as if what they're seeing was somehow inevitable, or a thing that the artist knows. But it's actually gone down this other track, this other way.

ANNIE DORSEN: Right. I mean, one thing that happens in art, of course, is that there's another element to the scientific method that we talked about, which is the notion of control. So if you're taking a stab at something and you're saying, "Well, what happens if I introduce this element?," you have to also see what happens if you don't introduce that element. And that can't relate. That is what we lack in artistic research: there is no such thing as control.

ELODIE GHEDIN: Oh, right.

ANNIE DORSEN: Because aesthetics are so slippery; they're so complex. There's so much nuance. Things that are accidental seem intentional when the audience sees them. Things that are almost uncontrollable by the performer—a little bit louder or a little bit less loud, or they move to the right instead of the left, whatever it is that happens in the moment of performance—all of those things go into the experience of the audience, and you can't really pin down exactly what collection of subtleties produces a certain effect. Not to mention how many different impacts, let's say, work can have—as many as there are people in the audience. Which, you know, when you're trying to identify the gases in the atmosphere, it's going

for something somewhere on the verge of realization,

to pretty much be the same every time. So that notion of replicability is also a question that I have about—

PETER N. MILLER: So, Annie, can I ask you, though, with the algorithmic theatre, do you ever think of it as a research project?

ANNIE DORSEN: Always. I always do, but then I wonder whether that's appropriate—also because I collaborate with computer scientists, and they have a totally different training in terms of what it means to do experiments, for example. So, I do very much think in terms of artistic research, and my projects are researches. There are also so many things we could talk about—how funding works and all that kind of stuff—because I have a premiere date before I've started a project, so you're kind of just hoping that the thing you've set out to do will turn out to be interesting. And then it often happens, to almost anyone who does performance, that there's a certain amount of scramble toward the end of the process to take all the stuff you've made and turn it into something that you hope means something to the audience. And there's something almost antithetical to the structure of making performance in the notion of research. You're kind of saying, "That's what I sort of feel like." There's a little bit where you have your fingers crossed behind your back while you talk about it, and you're kind of saying, "Well I'm doing a research. It's an exploration of a certain set of techniques, or it's a question. But at the same time I'm going to have an opening night coming, and I'm trying to make something good." And then you don't know what you—

CAMPBELL MCGRATH: You've got to put something up there opening night, whether you're sure of it or not.

ANNIE DORSEN: And then, all of a sudden, you're talking in terms

for what lies around the corner, five or six blocks uptown, of things like good and bad as opposed to, you know, interesting, producing new questions, or there's other adjectives that you might use if you're being strict with yourself or about the notion of "research." But in a certain moment, that performance necessity arises, and you do want that interaction with the audience. Maybe that's a better way of talking about good or bad: that with a good piece, there's a feeling of interaction. But I don't know, I mean, with a poet, of course, you're not there with the audience...

CAMPBELL MCGRATH: There's no deadlines, which is the best thing about poetry land. There's no funding, so therefore, no deadlines.

[*laughter*]

CAMPBELL MCGRATH: I mean, I never have a deadline, except for self-imposed ones, like, "I really want to finish this project up, and send it to my editor, and see what he says." So, that's very nice, you know? I mean, I know it doesn't feel nice for a long time, but you have to have a day job as a professor or what have you, because you're never going to get funded through the actual piece of writing. But I never have that moment of, "It is opening night, and the curtain's going to go up, and I have to put something up there." That's a very different kind of reality.

ANNIE DORSEN: And then, of course, this whole aesthetic has kind of arisen in response to all these questions, where there's sort of a notion of people showing their research as the work. This is much more common in visual art than in performance, but it's still pretty common in performance. And I always wonder, "But is it real research, or is it kind of an illusion of realism?" Like, the real thing, or is it gussied-up research?

hiding out in the Bronx or across the river in Jersey.

CAMPBELL MCGRATH: Right. That's interesting.

ANNIE DORSEN: And I don't know, maybe something similar happens in your field.

ELODIE GHEDIN: Well, I guess that's what happens when you put your methods in scientific papers, or the story. When you write a scientific paper, you always have a story, and it's got a beginning, a middle, an end. But, in fact, it all happened in a jumble, and actually when you have baby scientists, who are these students—when they write, they write chronologically, and it makes no sense, but it's chronological. And you say, "No, you make a story—a story." And actually, physicists—theoretical physicists—always say, "What is wrong with you biologists? You always want to have a story. You don't need a story." But, yeah, I think we need a story if we want to do the outward-facing thing and communicate our science. And that's one thing we often don't do very well. We don't communicate our science very well. That's why, you know, there are all these vaccine controversies, and people doubt the scientific method. And, I think, in general, the training in the US—sadly, even in high school—you don't get exposed to what science means. And so, people don't believe in science. They think it's a belief, and you're like, "No, it's not a belief. It's just facts or no facts." Right? So I think that's part of the issue, and that's why we have to communicate really well.

CAMPBELL MCGRATH: So, I made the assertion that, for me, loafing on the beach and digging up seashells is a form of research. And I'm not a scientist of seashells or beaches; I write poetry. But if walking on the beach picking up seashells is the way of opening your soul to be a crucible, or letting the non-agendized, non-structured, non-research—no, a better word would be, maybe, non-scripted—way of the world and of you to interact, then that's a very, very vital form of research.

Somewhere on the streets of the city right now somebody

I just wonder if any of you have a fellow feeling of that, or if I've just devised a clever definition of research to allow myself to go to the beach and describe it as research.

[*laughter*]

SHEILA NIRENBERG: I think it's research. Anything that provokes new thinking. Because part of research is that first inspiration to do something. I mean, something happens and you have a thought, and then you write a poem. I think that's the same thing as having an idea and doing a set of experiments. I mean, not the same, but it has the same structure. I think you're fully justified in calling that research.

TOM JOYCE: And nothing remains the same, you know? Each one of the walks reveals something else, right? Yeah. I love comparative study—you know, where you have multiples of many different forms, but of, like, type.

HIDEO MABUCHI: Yeah, I mean, I definitely think that sort of thing is research. For me, the biggest advances that you make are when you kind of take apart the old framework of something—of the way that you thought about something—and see the possibility of a new one. But in order to do that, you have to be in a place where you can let go of a bunch of immediate priorities. And that's hard. You know, just professionally, that's a hard thing to do. There's always some to-do list that you're trying to deal with, and what you need in order to have the kind of insight—or just an idea, or an inkling of something that takes you somewhere new—you need to get all that to-do list stuff out of your head. So whatever way you have of doing that is really an important—

is meeting the love of their life for the very first time,

TOM JOYCE: Yeah. Breathing room.

AN-MY LÊ: Well, I think that it's important to have the rigor to know your medium, to understand your techniques. And that confidence allows you to be flexible—to take risks and play. That's what I mean when I think, as a visual artist, that anything goes. And I think doing the research and knowing as much as I can on the subject before I embark on a trip is also important. Knowing how it's been photographed, and asking if there's room for more pictures. Like looking at *National Geographic* to know the difference between what an art photographer would do on an aircraft carrier, and what you would find in *National Geographic*.

PETER N. MILLER: Terry?

TERRY PLANK: As for rigor, well, we're scientists—we have to be rigorous. And I guess I'm quite a stickler about this. I had a friend, a Russian, who said, "Terry, our paper, it's like a bridge. You have to stand under the bridge and make sure it doesn't fall." I always think of this when we write papers. It's pushing the extra 80% to finish all the details, to make sure it's a good piece of work—data, interpretation, model that anyone would come up with—and that I'd be willing to stand underneath the bridge. This is something I impress upon my students, and probably to their detriment. I don't publish a lot of papers, but you hope they stand up. So that's what resonated here. No imagination in what I do…

PETER N. MILLER: We'll come back to that in a second.

TERRY PLANK: It's persistent driving.

MARINA RUSTOW: I was actually going to ask both of you how you define rigor, and then, how you define imagination. But if you want to avoid answering that, I'm happy to just answer the question.

PETER N. MILLER: No, no. I think that's a really good question.

MARINA RUSTOW: I mean, so I'll just throw in my two cents, and then I'd like to hear what you have to say about that.

TERRY PLANK: Yeah, it's easy for you to push the question off.

[*laughter*]

MARINA RUSTOW: So, rigor is absolutely fundamental also to what historians do. And this is why I've embraced the label of philologist—although I think many historians who work with obscure, or difficult, or dead languages are somewhat embarrassed by the whole philology thing. You know, it's very dry, and philologists are in the business of publishing texts. But we interpret texts, we historians. I embrace the whole philology thing because I think that's really the fundament of writing plausible history. But at the same time, the rigor, and the philology, and the technical skills without the imagination is totally pointless.

　　I also gain a lot of intellectual inspiration from making things with my hands. I teach a course on the material culture of medieval Cairo, where I invite a paper maker to come and make paper in the medieval style with my students. For me, it's not until I throw myself into a situation as much as possible that I start asking the right sorts of questions. Imagination, for me, is very literal—in that I have to be doing, in order to have the capacity to imagine. But, at the same

discussing Monty Python with a man impersonating a priest,

time, I would say that rigor and imagination are not really so separate, in the sense that it's precisely in the rigorous process of trying to understand what you don't know that the imagination starts to work. In yoga, they say you have to go down to come up—like you can't jump high unless you have a deep bend to spring from. It's like that.

PETER N. MILLER: So now, I want to take Marina's question and pose it to you, Terry. You way too modestly said just now, "No, no, no, not me." But, let's take an example like experiment design, right? What's the role of imagination there?

TERRY PLANK: I don't know; it's not going to resonate in experimental design. You try something and it doesn't work, and then you try something else and it doesn't work, and then you try a third something and it doesn't work. To me, there is so much of it that's persistence. You could imagine something clever, but it usually doesn't work. And then you've got to try again. So I often feel like a lot of what we do is persistence. You know, I'm trying to think about where this imagination comes in, and imagination to me is like the driving dream. It's what I would like to imagine, because so much of what we do we can't see. Like, what is happening under the volcano? What the hell is a subduction zone? I have this dream of being able to walk into the earth and finally see what the plate is doing.

Our field is full of ridiculous cartoons of what's under a volcano—you know, giant vats of magma, or thin sheets, or columns of mush. Seriously, you can get this stuff published in *Nature*—a stupid cartoon under a volcano. But there is an aspect of what drives us and what is, I suppose, a notion of what's happening that requires a leap of imagination and faith in what's happening under the earth.

PETER N. MILLER: I'm going to push one more button and extra-

someone is waiting for the bus to South Carolina

polate from what Marina said about the collision of the rigor and the imagination, and say that where it happens is in the question that emerges. So, Terry, where do your questions come from?

TERRY PLANK: They're super basic. I'm sorry. Again, we are such a young field; it's not complicated. It's like, "Why is this eruption more explosive than that of ten years ago?" Seriously, we have to ask the most fundamental questions. Like, "Where does the magma come from? What is the pacing of processes that makes magma?" These are really just fundamental questions that we still don't know the answer to.

AN-MY LÊ: But what about the role of intuition? Because you talk about how little is known, and so, yes, you ask these basic questions. But to even know where to navigate within that big dark zone is...

MARINA RUSTOW: What about hypotheses? Are hypotheses the product of imagination? Would you like to lie down on the couch? We can analyze you.

[*laughter*]

TERRY PLANK: Maybe for some people. For me, they're like, again, the most basic question. You can spend a lot of time working on little questions, OK. And so, honestly, it's like, work on the big question: "Why is the volcano erupting crazy? What controls the explosive behavior of volcanoes?" It is a question that most people are not squarely facing. They're like, "Why is the lava runny today?" But it's not centrally focused on the question that we care about, and I think that's where most of my hypotheses are.

to visit her sister in hospice, someone is teleconferencing

MARINA RUSTOW: I'll just chime in on that and say that I also find that the most difficult questions to answer are the simplest ones. Questions like, "Where did people cook their food?" You'd think there would be obvious answers to that, because in the culture that I study, they do it twice a day. It's something so pervasive, and yet it's taken us a really long time to even have a viable hypothesis about it. Whereas, you know—

TERRY PLANK: And you're the only person asking this question.

MARINA RUSTOW: I'm one of maybe three.

TERRY PLANK: Right.

MARINA RUSTOW: But, yes. The basic questions are really hard to answer.

PETER N. MILLER: An-My, can we now go back to rigor?

AN-MY LÊ: Well, I think rigor for a visual artist is about understanding the medium and the materiality. Are you using the right tool? If you're interested in this, should you use a small camera? Should you have grainy prints? Should you use artificial lighting? What kind of tool would you be using? And so I think knowing all of that and not being scared of the hard work—if it requires a larger camera or such and such—is important. I think there is a kind of rigor in pursuing things to the end. You know, photography is so easy; anyone can take a picture, right? Yes, you can photograph around you, but is that really significant? It could be, but I mean, maybe it's not, and maybe it requires you to travel, or ask for access, or not. I think those are all questions to consider and to push yourself.

with the office back in Hartford, Antwerp, Osaka,

I think it's very easy to be lazy as a photographer.

MARINA RUSTOW: Embedding yourself, I mean—that's a form of rigor, right? Spending three and a half weeks on an arctic ship, that's a form of rigor, right? You're—

AN-MY LÊ: Or masochism.

MARINA RUSTOW: Isn't it the same thing?

AN-MY LÊ: And, you know, deep down you keep thinking there is this theory that we have as photographers that you should not be a tourist photographer. You know, that the simple equivalence would be going to India, and being so taken up by all the colors, but staying on the surface of things. To be able to get past that, you need to have some kind of personal connection, or really spend a lot of time somewhere and immerse yourself in that. But it's not always true. I mean, I've done that so much, and now I can actually walk into a place and have two hours, and sometimes come out with a good picture. And I feel a bit like a fraud. But maybe it's because I did all that work before.

PETER N. MILLER: What do you have now that lets you do the work in two hours?

AN-MY LÊ: I think it's sensing the opportunities. And when something doesn't present itself as you had imagined, not to get all shaken up. Because it's the things you don't expect that are the most surprising. And so I look for something else. Don't be disappointed and go, "I have done that in the past." And you always find something else. It's also about asking. I used

someone is dust-sweeping, throat-clearing, cartwheeling,

to be afraid of asking—"Oh, can you do that again?," or "Can you stand over here?"—because you don't want to interrupt. So, it's doing all those things.

PETER N. MILLER: Terry, when you go to a new volcano, do you have certain kinds of things you're always going to look for?

TERRY PLANK: Certainly. As scientists, we have to have training and develop our eye. It is especially tricky in geology to develop an eye for what kind of rock this is. I have to say, students usually panic when you first give them a rock. They're like, "Oh my god, it's just a rock." It's like, "Take a deep breath. Does it have bubbles? Does it have crystals?" So, there is certainly an aspect of developing an eye. I actually am not a volcanologist, even though I'm studying volcanoes. The real volcanologists are the people who map deposits. They go after the eruption or during the eruption and map what it did—the lava flows, the air fall.

Description: Micro-CT scan (X-ray tomography) of an olivine crystal (approx. 1 mm) from the 1957–2. eruption of Quizapu Volcano in Chile. The red blebs are blobs or magma (now frozen as glass) that were trapped inside the crystal as it grew. Courtesy of T. Plank.

I'm trying to learn to do this since I never really learned that in graduate school. I learned the chemistry of the lavas and the chemistry of the gases. So, it's pretty exciting to go into the field with somebody who is an expert in this and work on Mount Etna. It's a great laboratory volcano—Etna having been studied well. We were trying to identify a deposit from an eruption in 2015. It's one of the most photogenic plumes you've ever seen—this huge column of ash that went up in still air, and then spread a mushroom cloud over Catania. And it leaves a deposit that's a few inches thick, and that was 2015.

knife-grinding, day-trading, paying dues, dropping a dime,

There have been a few eruptions since then, so if you needed to go and identify exactly that deposit, you had to take an expert in the field who knew which way the wind was blowing subsequently, and which deposits had been on top of the other. We literally dug a pit, and closed our eyes, and felt for the parting between the layers. There is definitely a lot of training that goes into what we do, and it's fun to learn these new tools later in your career.

PETER N. MILLER: So, Marina, do you also have a kind of two-minute drill for seeing a problem and figuring out how you want to tackle it?

MARINA RUSTOW: Yes, and I spend a lot of time trying to actually articulate what the drill is. So, I am advising a couple of juniors at Princeton for their junior papers, which is like a mini senior thesis. And one of them wants to write on documents from the cache that I work on, but that are in Ladino—meaning they're from a later period, basically after 1391, which is the first big wave of Jewish exiles from the Iberian Peninsula. There was a Spanish-speaking community in Cairo starting in 1391 and it grew.

And in the 16th and 17th centuries, it was quite prominent and quite large, but very few people have actually worked on the Ladino—or Judeo-Spanish—documents from this cache. They've just been totally ignored in favor of the earlier stuff. I now have a student who knows Spanish and knows how to read Hebrew script. She emailed me in a panic last week because she can't read the stuff. What to do? First, I said, "Take a deep breath. Let's sit down together, and we'll look at it." In fact, it was a type of Hebrew handwriting that I myself had really no experience reading. I was paying close attention to how I was actually able to work my way around this. Essentially, you know, there are certain key things that you can do.

giving the hairy eyeball, pissing against a wall,

One: the first word of a document is always absolutely crucial. In the ones that she was looking at, two of the three happened to begin "Señor" and "Señora," from which we knew they were letters. So that was really exciting, because then you know what to expect. A lot of deciphering is about creating a set of expectations based on clues, like any detective work, and then maybe sometimes working against those expectations where they're not panning out. But I will say, there is quite a bit of connoisseurship involved, and that annoys me.

There are probably some art historians sitting here who know what I mean. You just have to see a lot of Rembrandts. And it's actually true—you just have to look a lot, and your eye will unconsciously pick up so much. And then the question is, how do you make that teachable? How do you make it kind of scientific? How do you impart it to students, and speed up the process of their seeing so many Rembrandts?

PETER N. MILLER: That was about research and rigor. Can we turn the coin over now? How do you place the word "research" vis-à-vis curiosity, imagination, and play?

HIDEO MABUCHI: With research in the sciences, you often begin by coming up with an idea that you want to be true. And so there's a major component of imagination and creativity there—coming up with something interesting that's possibly true, that you want to be true. But then the rigor in it comes in, and you say, it's another thing to really prove something to a reasonable scientific standard. The rigor is there so that you don't fill the literature with a lot of things that are false. And so then, when you go back and try to prove that guess— either through rigorous experimentation or through some rigorous mathematical procedure—you know when you do prove it, that you can stand on that, and move on. But what's even more interesting is when you prove that you were wrong

someone is snoozing, sniffling, cavorting, nibbling,

in your initial guess. Because then you have to go back and figure out, "Why was my intuition off? How do I go back and reorient everything that I thought I knew so the next time I make a guess it will be better?" I think that interplay is something at the same time both imaginative and rigorous. That, I think, at least on the scientific side of things, is the method that people follow.

TOM JOYCE: Well, I was actually wanting to ask you a question as far as you're inside the scientific community. Cyril Stanley Smith, the great metallurgist and metal historian, talks about the fact that so much that drives science was actually developed long before, through the curiosity that one would find inside a workshop—or to put it another way, in a space outside scientific thinking. Science really is building on that— the curiosity of people outside the field. I'd like to know how much of what you're deciding to investigate is self-generated, or is being generated by others feeding the curiosity inside yourselves.

SHEILA NIRENBERG: I think, for me, because I wasn't a biology major and I came into it from a different field, I was freer in a way from the constraints of what everybody else knows and how everybody else does things. I just did it my way, and I didn't worry about it too much. I mean, I occasionally embarrassed myself, but mostly it was worth it, and that allows you to make connections that other people wouldn't make. And I think that helps. But it's the same idea—I was the outsider... And listening to other people, too. Actually being engaged in a conversation and not just pontificating. And I know, we're doing pontificating right now, but... [*laughing*]... because really good scientists, I find, always are good listeners also. Conversations have to be two-way. You never know where something is going to lead.

I do want to say something, though, that's unrelated, but comes back to something you were saying before about

roistering, chiding, snuggling, confiding,

how you get invested in your own hypothesis. You know, it's just human nature that you really want something to be true. You're proud of your idea. I always hedge my bets so I can get invested in two different things. Like, I have two different companies. And so, you don't depend, like we do as scientists, on writing one grant. And so have two grants—or in your grant, propose alternative ideas. That way you don't get so stuck that you have to force some answer. Being in a bind is what makes you a bad scientist.

HIDEO MABUCHI: I spend a lot of time these days thinking about the connection and the lack of connection between modern science and traditional craft. When I interact with the community of potters—people who know clay, and they know firing clay—they know a lot, but it's about how to get the results they want in their finished work. They have an extreme, intuitive understanding of the material and the firing process. But then, when you start to talk to them about why things are the way they are—like, "Why does this color appear?," or "What's going on in your kiln when you do this with the chimney?"—often the explanations that come out don't make any sense. And maybe that doesn't really matter. It starts to matter when people are not working with their own clay and their own kiln, but are going somewhere else in the world and trying to work with somebody else's clay and somebody else's kiln.

The big change is that modern science is based on abstraction and theoretical understandings of things, and that has a certain power, but it's limited. When I'm interested in the physics of ceramics, I rely on the many generations of people working in traditional craft, and the interesting phenomena that they have discovered. And it's only because we have those very interesting phenomena to try to explain that there's anything to do, even, as a physicist coming into a field like that. But then, a thing that I think has struck me most in my professional career for the past few years is, I've started teaching introductory ceramics classes for students. The

pub-crawling, speed-dating, pump-shining, ivy-trimming,

difference between that teaching experience versus getting up in front of a lecture and talking about physics for a while—it's such a difference—and I think the thing that is really awesome is that when you're teaching students how to center clay on a potter's wheel, the first questions that always come out of the Stanford students are, "Am I doing this right?" and "What's the next step?" It makes you realize that the way that we teach these physical sciences or mathematics, it's so, like, "Here are the things you need to know. Here are the problems you need to solve. And then, if you can do that, you get an A." Whereas with something that is much more material-based, I love to tell them, "There's nothing I can tell you that's going to make you a better potter. You just have to put in the time to develop your own kinetic relationship with this material and this tool. Put in the time and you'll get it." And I think there's actually something extremely valuable in that, that we've lost from the way that we tend to teach science. This kind of knowledge that comes from familiarity with material is a really critical thing for science. We don't teach it very well.

PETER N. MILLER: Would you call that research?

HIDEO MABUCHI: Yeah. I mean, the thousands of hours you need to put in to really be comfortable throwing clay—that's research. It's for yourself; it's not something that you can easily share with others, but it feels the same.

But I want to jump back to this question about research, and the term, and ask, if you broaden it to include so much, then what's the use of having the term anymore? Because it really reminds me of things that I read when people are talking about, "What is art?"—that if you just say, "Everything is art," then what's the point of having that category? And I found myself very sympathetic to approaches that people will take to say that, "OK, 'What is art?' is maybe not the right question. The right question is, 'When is art?'"

tap-dancing, curb-kicking, rat-catching, tale-telling,

And so I think you could do a similar thing with research—that, yes, sometimes when you're surfing the web, you really are just goofing around and killing time. But there are occasions on which you'll be doing something that you really want to think of as research—that is methodologically indistinguishable from research.

PETER N. MILLER: Tom, you were going to say something before?

TOM JOYCE: Well, I was actually just thinking about throwing off the hump, you know. But it's really—it would be more tied to an embodying, a kind of process that allows memory and your cognitive abilities to be able to recreate something over, and over, and over. Throwing off the hump is where you take a larger lump of clay, and you put it on the wheel, and you throw small cups only out of the top portion of it. And because you are pulling a bowl or a cup out of it—cutting it off, setting it aside, and then you have the clay body of sufficient quantity enough to be able to pull another bowl or another cup off of it—sometimes you pull twenty cups, and it's the easiest way to be able to have something come out more uniformly than doing it one at a time. But it also teaches a kind of embodiment of those techniques, so as a research facilitator, embodying that through the memory of repetition is key.

getting lost, getting high, getting busted, breaking up,
breaking down, breaking loose, losing faith,
going broke, going green, feeling blue, seeing red,
someone is davening, busking, hobnobbing, grandstanding,
playing the ponies, feeding the pigeons, gull-watching,
wolf-whistling, badgering the witness, pulling down the grill
and locking up shop, writing a letter home in Pashto or
Xhosa, learning to play the xylophone, waiting for an Uber X,
conspiring, patrolling, transcending, bedeviling,
testifying, bloviating, absolving, kibitzing,

IV.

PETER N. MILLER: I think between imagination and curiosity, we lost "play." Can I ask you now to focus on it?

TERRY PLANK: Play? I like to teach my students to own the data. They've collected their data on their volcanic rocks. They're looking at the chemistry. I want them to own it—to know every data point, every rock, the weird outliers, the ones that are totally normal—and to try and see the systematics in the data that way. Too often they just kind of want to throw it in a statistics package. And to still get very personal with data that you've collected. It's hard to collect. We have to get the sample, we have to grind it up, we have to go in the lab, we analyze it—each data point is hard won. And I want the students, and myself, to own the data and then see the beauty with either the systematics in it or what's not working.

PETER N. MILLER: An-My, how do you teach them to play?

AN-MY LÊ: Well, usually, I tell the student to try to play if I feel they're too stuck or too rigid, or if they have been too serious and they were working on a project too long and just need a break. I would tell them to use a video camera and switch from still to moving image. If they're using a small camera, I would tell them to pick up a heavier camera, like an 8×10, or a 4×5 view camera, or an iPhone—to just relax and try something else. You always try to get them out of whatever it is that they are stuck in.

MARINA RUSTOW: I just figured out my answer. So, basically, writing historical novels is how I get students to play. I mean, having them do that. A few years ago, my colleague

kowtowing, pinky-swearing, tarring and shingling,

at Princeton, Eve Krakowski, and I had to design a set of general exam questions for some PhD students. And I don't know what got into us; we were feeling bored and silly. And so we painted a scenario. We were like, "OK, your name is 'X' and you're a Jew living in 11th century Cairo. Your business partner has just walked off with all the capital that you invested in a deal in Yemen. Your wife has just left you. Your son has trashed your house." I mean, these are all real scenarios from letters that we've read. We essentially painted this whole scenario, and we asked the students, "What do you do?" And it's fascinating actually to see them write their way out of this. We got two answers from the two students we inflicted this on that were so totally brilliant, to the point where they were kind of cracking in-jokes about the existing scholarly literature between the lines. It was so great, and at that point, we realized they were totally ready to write a dissertation. I would say that was a breakthrough for us as teachers.

TERRY PLANK: Yeah, next time they could write a country song about that...

PETER N. MILLER: Sheila, if a caricature of scientific method would be a version of Caro's "turn every page," then I'm wondering, where does the play come in?

SHEILA NIRENBERG: I would just answer it a little bit off-angle from what you're asking. So, first of all, I wasn't always a scientist. I was an English major in college and I wanted to be a writer. So, I start big picture, and just drill all the way down. But that's very different from the scientist who starts drilling and then looks for a reason to have drilled. Forgive that— arrogant, saying it that way. But we've all gone to seminars that are like that—you know what I mean. I think that, just related to what you were saying before, the creative process

breaking and entering, delivering and carting away,

happens partly when you solve a problem. Like a math problem, I always solve it geometrically first, so I can see the relationship. And then you go back into the algebra to figure out if you are actually right. There's a lot of mathematicians claiming they solved it by doing the proof, and they came out with the answer. It never happens that way. I would really bet a lot of money that no one has ever actually solved a problem that way. There is an artistry to it: you see relationships among things, and then you try to formalize it. That's where the turning of the page comes—it's to make sure that what you see is not an illusion of a relationship, but a true relationship. And that's where the discipline comes in—to do the algebra and see if you're right.

TOM JOYCE: Well, I would say that sometimes there's that leap, too, that allows one to not move in this circuitous way, but a more direct line, and then prove the theory based on this visualization that came, you know, maybe in those last waking moments as you're heading to sleep—

SHEILA NIRENBERG: Yeah, right.

TOM JOYCE: —which is often that moment that you relax to the degree that there's spaciousness around your thought processes, to be able to solve problems. You know, I was also really taken recently with a book by James Hillman—it's really a collection of his essays on alchemical psychology. And he makes a reference to the fact that all of what the creative process is revolving around is this kind of cooking process, the same as the alchemist working on distillation, and putrefaction, and pickling, and all of those aspects of what would go on in the laboratory. It's a process of working in an evaporative way to be able to find the kernel, the nugget, the solid evidence at the end of that, you know, funnel-shaped distillation. And I think that's what you all

enwreathing lampposts with yellow ribbons,

must deal with also in the laboratory, when you're thinking outside the box. It's something that comes in unexpected ways, but is just hammered out—like you say, drilling down.

CAMPBELL MCGRATH: I want to go back to that Whitman thought about "loafing and inviting the soul." Because that word "loafing"—that can get you in trouble, because sometimes you do loaf. But to loaf and invite the soul is different, because to invite the soul is really rigorous, and hard, and actually kind of scary. I mean, it's actually researching something that isn't easily put into a formula—or even thought about. The Greeks spent a lot of time trying to pin it down and put it in your liver or your pancreas. "Where is it? It's there, but where is it?" And then Wittgenstein said, "Well, we can't talk about it, but that doesn't mean it doesn't exist." Because we all understand there is a soul. There's something that makes you "you"—something that happens when we die. We aren't just the biological mechanism, and we aren't just our minds, as brilliant as they are. There's some other kind of weird...—I don't want to say magical, but mysterious—reality that tends to get labeled the "soul." But since the term has no real meaning, a thousand different thoughts are attached to it. "To loaf and invite the soul" is, I think, a very traditional poetic for something the poets often take as their particular research domain and philosophers do from a different direction.

But that can be playful. And that's about play and curiosity. There can be a dark night of the soul, or if you really get into the soul. The poet Li-Young Lee is like, "You've got to travel into the heart of the volcano to get at certain material." And I think that's really true. And that's a dangerous place to travel to, and so you need to have an asbestos suit or just get out of the volcano really quickly. But what if the thing your poetry points you towards entails going into part of the volcano for a long time? It's like, there are certain dangers. I don't want to over-dramatize them, but again, that "loafing and inviting the soul" is often playful, and quixotic, and episodic, and about curiosity and the way it just intuitively

reading Apollinaire on a bench littered with fallen petals,

wanders through the world. But it can have a kind of rigor of the kind of dark night of the soul that takes you to dark places.

So for me, these terms, again, overlap. Because different kinds of poems entail, for me, different kinds of research—from the kind of really rigorous, intellectual, archival research which happens sometimes, to, "Oh, this particular seashell—I love it. What is it? Let's now go to our seashell book and look it up," and follow that, to thinking about language and following language down its paths. But there's a kind of rigor, even to the loafing—if your loafing is actually intended to invite the soul. That's a method, too.

ELODIE GHEDIN: You know, a lot of what we do is try things often. So yeah, we're following a method—a scientific method. We have controls, we have statistical significance, but then we also do a lot of, "Let's try putting this with these cells and see what happens." We do that a lot—like it's a chemistry set. And I have to say, that's when we have fun, and we do see things we didn't expect, and we pursue those. Then we'll move it into, "OK, let's do a real experiment." We do a lot of these preliminary experiments, or just for fun. And it is fun, and we get all excited. "Ooh, I tried this, I discovered that." There's a lot of that, too, in science.

PETER N. MILLER: Would you call that play?

ELODIE GHEDIN: Yes! I mean, it is kind of play, actually. I have one particular student who is really imaginative, and he'll say, "I want to try this." Or he'll do something and he'll say, "I tried something just for fun." That's what we call it. And then it's great. Now, we do things to play. Scientists often are big babies. You get us all together—especially biologists, who do a lot of computational work—and it seems to become some type of mix where they're like kids. They're always playing, and you have to amuse them. So, we have a lot of competitions of whatever, you know? For a while we had a competition where we had the "Wall of Shame," where you'd have to post the worst experiment you've ever had so everybody could see your lousy experiment. Or we'll do these competitions which we call "Lab Project Runway," where you have to make outfits with discarded things from the lab. And these scientists go completely crazy for that.

So, yes, there is a lot of play there, but it's still important for the research, because when we play like that, we end up talking, and then we communicate with each other, and we get ideas we want to try. I know that's not what you meant by play, but it's sort of the mentality you have that really leads you that way. My husband is an MD, and when he comes to my conferences, he's like, "Oh my god, you're all batshit crazy—all of you." And I go to his conferences, I'm like, "Oh my god, they're so boring." It's a completely different world, you know?

ANNIE DORSEN: I'm kind of relieved to hear this, because I had this thought from a book by James Bridle—who's an artist who writes about computation and stuff—where he has a whole chapter about how computation has killed the spirit of play and free inquiry in science. And—

ELODIE GHEDIN: Oh, no... That's not... not the computational people I deal with. Yes... There's an aspect of computation that can be soul-crushing, right? But I think it's—

ANNIE DORSEN: That's the one I go right towards.

[*laughter*]

toward home. No wonder they fear it so intensely,

ELODIE GHEDIN: But it's completely cross-disciplinary. And I think that it's at that intersection where you get people who like to play. Because just the fact that you're crossing this barrier makes it more interesting.

ANNIE DORSEN: I'm very comfortable with the notion of curiosity, and I'm much less comfortable with the notion of play. And I think it's because I come from theatre, where there's so much nonsense about "play." It's all very froofy. And I always felt in theatre class that I didn't know how to play correctly. The whole concept stresses me out.

ELODIE GHEDIN: So, what is play in theatre? When you...

ANNIE DORSEN: In real, like, normal theatre?

ELODIE GHEDIN: Yeah, what you would call normal. When you say you don't like play, what is play in that context?

ANNIE DORSEN: I mean, it's—

ELODIE GHEDIN [*to audience*]: She just rolled her eyes! I mean...

[*laughter*]

ANNIE DORSEN: I know there are some amazing clowns, and there are some amazing actors who really do seem to have this spirit of complete freedom in their imaginations, and it's really fantastic when people are good at it. But I had a little bit of an allergy to it, and I think I do the thing that is known

the ideologues and isolationists in Kansas and Kandahar, it is a

as play, but I have to, like, trick myself. I have to come in through the side or something, because otherwise I get too stressed about it.

PETER N. MILLER: So to de-stress you, let me ask the question to you in a slightly different way. With the *Hamlet* machine, if you had set out to use the algorithmic approach to explore all of the linguistic possibilities in the play other than the ones that Shakespeare decided to do, how would that be different from the actual play that you produced?

ANNIE DORSEN: But that's kind of what we did. So one thing that I always lead with is that, normally, I work with very simple algorithms for the most part—not the cutting edge of computer science in any way. In fact, like miles away from it. And that's very much on purpose, because I like to be able to understand what the algorithms are doing. And I even like that when you watch a piece, if you have no computer science background whatsoever, you could reverse engineer in your mind what the algorithm is doing. Because I like to demystify these things so it doesn't look like, "Ooh, cool effects and magic." So, I was using this very simple Markov chain, which is just a really simple sequencing algorithm. It's a famous algorithm that's used for lots of stuff. It's dumb—it's completely dumb. The computer scientists I worked with thought, "Why do you want to do that?" And then we did a couple of more sophisticated things, but that's it. I mean, it is—it is play—and it is about finding out what kinds of linguistic combinations arise, or how new poetry can be developed when you set parameters that are looser or tighter on what the computer can give you. "When does it start getting boring?" is a question. Does it get boring and then get interesting again? When do you start to project onto the computer system some idea of inner life? You start to imagine that the computer is wanting something, or feeling something. All of these things were

questions, and so we are experimenting around
the difficulties.

PETER N. MILLER: And Elodie, with the influenza virus, where
you're trying to map the constantly changing cosmos of
influenza viruses, is it similar to what Annie was talking
about? That, in a way, you're trying, through the repetition
or the capturing of these variations on the main theme,
to understand what the Influenza Virus is—with a capital
"I" and a capital "V," as in the Platonic form of the influenza
virus—in the same way that we're learning something
about the possibilities in Shakespeare by generating all of
these variations?

ELODIE GHEDIN: The comparison is not bad. Personally, in my
research, we don't do that exactly, but there is a field of
research specifically where they've noticed that the flu virus,
when you compare the proteins that the virus expresses on
its surface—that's what your immune system recognizes—
with all the flu viruses from the past, they've noticed that
actually there is a sort of a path. And so although we can't
really predict where it will go in the future, it seems to have
a limited sort of landscape that it can explore and still be
a viable virus.

To be more concrete: the flu virus replicates every
six hours, and will make one mistake per replication event,
per genome. OK? So that means it will make one mistake
every time. But you have millions of these viruses. That
means that the genome is only 10,000 letters long, and you
have millions of them. 90% of the genomes have a mutation,
and these mutations could lead to new proteins, basically.
That's the idea. Or different flavors of the protein that your
immune system doesn't completely recognize. But 90% of
those viruses are not viable either, because these mistakes
render them non-viable. And so there is a limit to where the
virus can evolve and change and mutate before it hits what's

a constant engagement with the shape-shifting mob,

called the "error catastrophe," where it disappears because it's too mutated. So, basically, it's the same idea, where you go through a path, constantly—

ANNIE DORSEN: Yeah, there's like a state space—

ELODIE GHEDIN: This space. And that's where the research is. What they're trying to do is understand that space better, and exactly where the limits are. What I do in my research is slightly different. We've noticed that in all that space you have what seems to be the dominant viruses, and then there are minor mutants that are there. And we've noticed that if we look at all that genetic diversity, we often see the diverse variant that will become the flu next season. We're trying to find it that way: to see by looking now if we can predict what will be the future.

Flu virus mosaic. Courtesy of E. Ghedin.

diversely luminous as sunlight reflecting off mirrored glass in puzzle pieces of apostolic light. Certainly this is not the Eternal City but it is certainly Imperial, certainly tyrannical, democratic, demagogic, dynastic, anarchic, hypertrophic, hyperreal. An empire of rags and photons. An empire encoded in the bricks from which it was built, each a stamped emblem of its labor-intensive materiality, hundreds of millions barged down the Hudson each year from the clay pits of Haverstraw and Kingston after the Great Fire of 1835, a hinterland of dependencies,

V.

PETER N. MILLER: Sheila brought up conversation before. What's the role of conversation, in particular—or the unstructured, in general—in research?

SHEILA NIRENBERG: Well, it's the conversation that sparks ideas. And then, later on, when you're going to really follow through—research means following through, really—to take it away from the conversation that triggered the idea. And then you go back and you say, "OK, does that really make sense?" And then you figure out a way to see if it's really true. Maybe that is a fundamental thing that makes speculation different from research. It's the opinion section of the news, versus the news.

TOM JOYCE: When I began blacksmithing, I was in my teens and the profession had all but died out. After World War II, there were very few possibilities for smiths to continue making hand-forged objects. So, my peers—the ones who were my age—were voracious. They were looking at and trying to gain as much knowledge while some of the elders were still willing to share that information. The desire was to research, and to make available to us techniques that could just as easily be lost forever. Continuity is part of how these skills are passed on—through fathers, sons, daughters, and the direct experience of these techniques. The community of smiths in the 1970s and '80s, I would say, was an immense laboratory where we shared information on a regular basis every few months—twice or three times a year at the minimum. Getting together just to be able to share these techniques, to bring historic objects into the center, and be able to discuss the methodologies that might not be apparent just in looking at the object. And there's a lot of tricks of the trade, as you know. I feel like it was that generation of smiths that allowed artists and other practitioners with an interest in learning all these trades to be able to have access to that information. Were it not for that research core, I think a lot would have been lost in the interim.

HIDEO MABUCHI: If I could try to combine answers to a couple of things that you just raised? You asked, "Can anybody do research?" So, something I try to get across with my classes is that, in a certain sense, you're doing research every time you waste a few hours surfing the web. Because if you just do this business about going to a page, clicking on a link, and you go to a new page, and you click on another link—I mean, you are doing something that, to me, is the core of research, because you are sorting your environment into things that are more interesting to you and less interesting to you, right? And, somehow, I think that's a fundamental aspect of what we call research. That's a thing you can do on your own. It's a thing that you can do in groups. You can collectively decide whether you're more interested in this thing or more interested in that thing. When it comes to trying to have the imagination to figure out a next step, or to find a technique that helps you rigorously prove something, that's obviously a situation in which you can pool resources. But to me, the one downer about trying to do research in a social setting is that all of this kind of curiosity-driven research is great as long as what you're interested in doing is not expensive, is not dangerous, and has no opportunity costs for other people. But a lot of the complication of the sociology of research comes with trying to justify why you're interested in doing some one thing and not some other thing. And then people start to ask, "Well, is it really worth it? What's it good for?" And then you kind of get into a whole other....

PETER N. MILLER: That's like the line between curiosity and research, right? That justification.

delivering serum to that muscular heart, a toiling collective

HIDEO MABUCHI: Umm, I don't know. I would take the purpose out of—I mean, maybe not everybody will agree—but I personally would want to take that practical purpose out of research. I just don't like that.

PETER N. MILLER: Do you work with this sort of polarity between—or dichotomy between—pure and applied research? Or do you not think in those terms at all?

SHEILA NIRENBERG: I mean, I do, but what I was doing first was basic science, so that's pure research. And then it led to a discovery, and then led to an application, two applications. So, it's a continuum. But purpose does matter, and I'm going to debate that with you.

HIDEO MABUCHI: Sure, sure.

SHEILA NIRENBERG: You know, I like to do it even if it turns out that the purpose was different from what I thought it would be. I feel the need to start with a reason. There are times when I can see completely why you're doing art or pottery, that you're just doing exploration. And in that sense, I can see not having the need for purpose, because the purpose may emerge from it. So, for example, I want to figure out how the brain works because people are so interesting. And so, yes, it is sort of a broad-strokes purpose of understanding the brain.

HIDEO MABUCHI: I think that in some corners of the physical sciences it is somewhat different. We're in an unusual situation, in that people don't like to talk about the fact that governments are not really funding basic research in the physical sciences anymore. All the money for really purely curiosity-driven, basic research in physics is gone. What there is instead

of Irish sandhogs and Iroquois beam walkers and Ivoirian

is a lot of applied research money, where people want to know how it is going to relate to innovation—I was wondering if that term was going to come up; I hate it—but they want to know, "How is this going to be good for technology? How is this going to increase the wealth of society, or impact society somehow?" I can't just say, "Well, look, here's something that feels like it's really core to the way we understand quantum mechanics, and we don't really understand it, so shouldn't we try to work it out?" But somebody would then say, "Oh, but how's that going to make better computers?" We always have to fall back on having that kind of justification in order to get funding for what we really want to do.

SHEILA NIRENBERG: It's starting to be the same thing in biology, too. It's about having a medical purpose. But—and don't anybody repeat this—but what you do is you write your grant on the main thing, and you work on that, and then you do a lot of experiments in the back room on the basic science part, because you have to understand it, fundamentally, to move it forward enough. If you're just throwing drugs at some disease, you're doing what those years of cancer research did that yielded nothing. You have to understand stuff. And so you can always siphon off a little bit... but don't report me or anything.

PETER N. MILLER: Do you think there's a difference between wanting to know, like, to know more, and doing research? I mean, reading lots of books, ingesting facts. Research or knowing?

TOM JOYCE: I don't. I see no separation whatsoever. Nor would I see a separation between cooking a meal and growing a garden, or doing art in a studio.

umbrella vendors collecting kindling for the bonfire

VI.

PETER N. MILLER: No one has mentioned yet the problem of failure. And I'm wondering if now would be a good time to ask each of you about the positive consequences of failure within research practice.

MARINA RUSTOW: The work-around can be very productive. I'd been trained to read Hebrew script documents, and it's actually much easier to do Hebrew paleography than Arabic paleography. Because Hebrew is an unconnected script, the handwriting can only get so bad. Arabic is a connected script, and in its documentary texts, writers tend not to use dots. And if you don't use dots for Arabic, you could look at a single symbol that could be one of five different letters. So, the complexity just multiplies. Confronted not only with things that I couldn't read, but also with things that were fragmentary, I realized that I wasn't going to be able to use the tools I was trained to use, which essentially amounted to decipherment until reaching a critical mass of information, and then writing history from that material. When I couldn't do that was when I started looking at more material clues, which is to say: paper, layout, the production of ink, and all the things that I actually could get a handle on when I couldn't read the text. And layout actually turned out to be a very productive line of inquiry, because I realized that I was interested in Arabic script documents and it turned out that many of the Arabic script documents were recycled for Hebrew script. And what's fascinating is that the first couple of generations who studied this material would publish the Hebrew script text and they wouldn't even see the gigantic line of Arabic across it. It's right there, you know? It's not like they couldn't see it. It's not a palimpsest where they've tried to erase it. But they didn't see it. It's just that mentally they were deleting the Arabic.

So, confronted with all these kinds of fragmentation,

that has lured, like moths, the entire world to its blaze.

I realized that if you were going to build a theory of where a given fragment must have come from, you just needed more evidence. That, for example, would let you distinguish between scribes who are working in the chancery issuing big public decrees versus the ones who are writing the tax receipts and not lifting the pen. In other words, I started trying to develop a visual typology of documents, precisely because I could not actually read the documents.

PETER N. MILLER: Terry, what about you?

TERRY PLANK: Again, I like to tell my students that if their experiment fails, they've actually learned something. If the instrument is working, they don't. And we have very sophisticated instruments. We're trying to melt rocks, or we're trying to measure parts per trillion of trace elements in species. When instruments fail and when experiments fail, I think the students at that point actually learn how the instrument is supposed to work. And they take ownership of the experiment and try something that's creative. That's when they're able to go off and run the instrument or their own experimental protocol. I think failures are where you learn.

PETER N. MILLER: And have you failed spectacularly in some case?

TERRY PLANK: I'm trying to think of a story. I don't know. Ask me over wine.

PETER N. MILLER: OK, An-My, what about failure?

AN-MY LÊ: I think not getting access has taught me a great lesson, and it's actually helped me build my work around that idea

As with my tree, the hubbub of bees its exaltation.

of what you do when you can't be in the front line. Which is what happened when I wanted to go to Iraq in 2003, and was put on the waitlist for an embed because I started too late. I discovered that the Marine Corps trains in a base outside of LA—hence this idea of photographing a copy of something, or photographing a re-enactment, photographing a film set. It was a way to tackle topical things without being right there and doing the things that a photojournalist would do so well. I think it taught me how to consider the secondary viewpoint of any big event, and how to make an interesting picture that would tackle the topic in a different way and say something different from what you would find in a newspaper, for example.

MARINA RUSTOW: Can I ask an unrelated question of An-My? I'm just dying of curiosity. You mentioned embedded photojournalists, although I guess it's a pretty new phenomenon. What about ethnography? Have you talked to anthropologists who do what they sometimes jokingly refer to as deep hanging out? Where you do something crazy like go on a ship for three and a half weeks or whatever, and you kind of have this unstructured process of just figuring stuff out by immersing yourself in details? Do you ever compare notes with people who do that kind of immersive fieldwork?

AN-MY LÊ: Yeah, I do. And it's fascinating. I mean, it's a bit like when you get a residency as a photographer. So, you go and photograph. As an architect, sometimes you get a residency and you can just say well, "I want to research these friezes," and then you just go, and you research. And it seems that I think it's such a bigger leap for them. I get something immediate with the photograph. And for them it's notes, and reflections, and long-term research.

Can I ask one question? Something I think a lot about in terms of the historian or visual artist versus the scientist is that, as a visual artist, you can actually spend a lot of time

Apis, *maker of honey,* Bombus, *the humble bumbler,*

doing research, and then completely throw it away. You can come up with something right there and then—a new work that has nothing to do with that research. And it's kind of astounding. You can't do that in history, or in science.

TERRY PLANK: To throw the research away, well, we just did. We just worked ten years measuring CO_2 in volcanic glasses. And we were measuring completely the wrong thing—not me, the whole community—and we helped show that it was wrong. So, that happens.

AN-MY LÊ: But you had to show that it was wrong?

TERRY PLANK: Yeah, we had to show it was totally wrong and own it—to say, "Yes, we've all been measuring the wrong thing. There is actually a bubble inside the crystal that has all the CO_2, and it's been hard to measure."

MARINA RUSTOW: But that's okay. I mean, that's changing your mind, which is different from throwing away research. Because you're still publishing a paper saying, "OK, we did that, but it's wrong," as opposed to doing a bunch of research and then you never publish the paper.

TERRY PLANK: Oh, I see.

AN-MY LÊ: Yeah, or doing something completely different.

PETER N. MILLER: Or, I think An-My's point was that you could do the research, thinking it was going to have one outcome, and then get rid of the research, and still do a thing that has

and the tree a common American beech.

an outcome. But it's tangential to the research, as if sparked by, but not its product.

TERRY PLANK: There is a lot of unpublished stuff languishing about, yes. Maybe it just isn't very exciting, so it didn't get published. I personally don't think I've ever thrown anything away. I'm afraid we're funded by the taxpayers, so that whatever we do, we should publish—even if it's wrong.

MARINA RUSTOW: I'll say that I started out as a historian thinking that, with all the research-y stuff, I needed to suppress it and put it in the footnotes, because I wanted to write a really flowing, wonderful narrative, so that even if you don't care about the archive, you'll care about my narrative. I approach it completely differently now. Now, I actually try to foreground the process of research within my historical narrative. Because it's precisely the kind of interaction between the struggles of the poor historian's brain and the recalcitrant material that, I think, actually fascinates people. I mean, what I always want to know about is what's going on behind the scenes. So, I would say that now I'm using all parts of the animal in a way that I wasn't when I started out. I was really leaving quite a bit out of the picture.

SHEILA NIRENBERG: Can I add to the discussion of failure? It's that failure is a big part of research. You have your idea, and you do an experiment, and it doesn't come out the way you think. You do the hand-waving and you make excuses for it, and you do it again, and you do it again, and after ten times, you realize, "I'm just freakin' wrong, and I have to accept it." You know, at first, you're incredibly miserable. And then slowly, you realize that that being wrong is actually a constraint that is telling you that the real hypothesis has to take into account that that wrong thing happened. And so suddenly you go from misery to the exhilaration of "I have a new idea." And you wouldn't have gotten there if you were always right about everything.

HIDEO MABUCHI: It's the only time you actually learn anything—right?—is when you fail.

SHEILA NIRENBERG: Right, exactly.

PETER N. MILLER: What are some other constructive failures? Can you think of other instances where you learned, let's say, as much from the failure as you had hoped from the success that didn't happen?

TOM JOYCE: Yeah, in the area of these industrial forges where I've been working, there are operators functioning at the cutting edge of technological innovation that has always played a role on the leading edge of iron being forged. And because of our dependence on iron, the failure rate in that industry cannot happen. They have to avoid it at all costs. So, as an artist and practitioner being given the privilege of working in that environment—it allows me to look at what they're really trying to avoid, and then to find some compelling evidence that would allow a different kind of investigation. And through that, there is a collaborative understanding that we're both testing the furthest reaches of what it is that we think this material is capable of doing. There's much more symbiosis than I thought possible, and the language we speak is really the same.

PETER N. MILLER: I was wondering if you have a personal practice that helps you maintain your own self-confidence.

hard against the wall of the Con Ed substation.

Forging at The Berg blacksmith shop. Anne-Marie Bouttiaux.

Along the fence some scraggly boxwood shrubs,

SHEILA NIRENBERG: Well, I'm going to answer it in a "science-y" way, with evidence to support it. This comes up especially with women—and I'm in a very, very male-dominated field—and so younger women will ask, "How do you have self-confidence?" You stand up straight, and you could wear shoes that make you taller, and talk in a deeper voice and all that. Or you could just do a lot of experiments, so that you have the confidence of the evidence. I work really hard, so that if I'm wrong, I have to have another idea, and now I have to prove that idea or test that idea so that when I go into a situation, I'm brave because I'm supported by evidence. When I give a seminar—in science, it's typically 50 minutes you have to talk, five–zero, and most people talk until the bitter end. What I try to do is just talk for 30 or 35 minutes at the most, and then let everybody ask me questions—just grill away. Because what I do covers gene therapy, and molecular biology, and neuroscience, and math, I want all those people who are skeptical to eventually say, "OK, OK, she answered that." And that's what gives me the confidence to accept failure. So if someone asks me a question, and I don't know, I say, "I don't know, but here's what I would do to test it." And you start to do it. Bullshitting just doesn't give you confidence; it makes you anxious and wanting to crawl into the closet. It's better to do as much as you can, so you can answer bravely. That's all we can do.

TOM JOYCE: I like that.

a table collapsed into rusted segments, two piles of bricks—
what's their story?—who made them, carted them,
set them as a patio, and who undid that work to create these
mundane, rain-eroded monuments to human neglect?
Why does nobody tend this little garden?
Undisciplined ivy scales the building in thick ropes
and coils of porcelain berry vine, whose fruit will ripen
to obscene brilliance come autumn, those strange berries,
turquoise, violet, azure... Ah, I've lost my train
of thought. Berries. The city. People, bricks, the past.

VII

PETER N. MILLER: Do you ever wish you could do a different kind of research? Like be a different kind of artist or scientist, and do research in a different way?

AN-MY LÊ: Well, I think I've always wanted to be a painter, but you start from scratch. It's really working from your imagination, or working from a photograph, or whatever. And I know how to do that. But I think the interesting thing is that, in the visual arts, when you do research, if you don't say that you're working from archives or working from ideas, there's some kind of stigma about not being intellectually rigorous. Vija Celmins, she's wandering around in her studio thinking about all kinds of great things—

PETER N. MILLER: Or Campbell McGrath on the beach—

AN-MY LÊ: —but you don't call that rigorous research. And that's something that I think about a lot. What does it mean to just be in your element, and doing your work, versus looking for ideas and being more intellectual about it?

PETER N. MILLER: Terry, other kinds of research you fantasize about doing?

TERRY PLANK: No, I love what I do. I have the best job in the world. When the MacArthur dude called out of the sky and said, "Here is a half million dollars. Now you can do what you've always wanted to do, like go play a violin." I'm like, "I don't play the violin. I love what I do, sorry. I have the best job in the world."

PETER N. MILLER: OK, Marina, ever fantasize about doing a different kind of research for a different kind of goal?

MARINA RUSTOW: I do fantasize often about doing other kinds of historical research, in two ways. One is it'd be nice to read manuscripts that are in English, say 19th-century letters.

TERRY PLANK: That's too easy.

MARINA RUSTOW: Yeah, exactly.

TERRY PLANK: It's like cheating.

MARINA RUSTOW: It's not hard enough.

TERRY PLANK: Yeah, right, exactly.

MARINA RUSTOW: It's not painful enough. The other thing I think about is, I have a friend who is from Venice who teaches at the University of Venice, and who writes about the history of Venice, and who goes to the archive on foot. And then I remember once passing a bookstore in Venice and seeing her book in the window and thinking to myself, "This is an experience that will never happen to me, where I live in the place on which I do research, and will see my book in a window in a shop in that place"—that kind of convergence. Whereas, here I am, in this ridiculous new world place, doing research on the most ancient country in the world, where all the sources are in Europe. It's so confusing! And I have no connection to Egypt. My father was from Berlin, grew up in Turkey, and moved to New York. I'm such a hodge-podge.

and permutations, viruses replicating, mutating, evolving.

It'd be so beautiful to have all things converge in that way.
But, then, I don't know, would I do what I do? I'm not sure.

Books in a library, bricks in a wall, people in a city.
A man selling old golf clubs on the corner of Ludlow Street.
A woman on the F train carefully rubbing ointment
up and down her red, swollen arms. Acorns—
tossing them into the Hudson River from a bench as I did
when I was Peter Stuyvesant, when I was Walt Whitman,
when we were of the Lenape and Broadway our hunting trail.
Then the deer vanished, the docks decayed, the towers fell.
The African graveyard was buried beneath concrete
as the memory of slavery has been obscured by metonymy

VIII.

PETER N. MILLER: I'm just thinking, what if we thought about research as something much more integral to self-formation or self-cultivation, as opposed to a pursuit of a kind of abstract goal outside of ourselves? What does that do to how we think about our institutions of learning, or the purpose of learning? Like, you were talking about the different kinds of classes you teach. Does something from research play out in the classroom?

SHEILA NIRENBERG: I'm a neuroscientist, too, so I'm interested in what we do and why we do it. And it's an endless source of questions. You answer one and then you realize you still need to follow it up with this one, and this one, and there are so many different directions. Maybe it's narcissistic that I do this, but we human beings are all so fascinating, and just trying to understand what things are inevitable. That is our stereotype: that we all make the same mistakes. What are the parts that are unique to us? What part of the neural activity makes it inevitable that a decision gets made? That keeps me going.

HIDEO MABUCHI: We were talking before this event started about the increasing digitalization and virtualization of knowledge and teaching, and the way that people relate to life and practical things, but this idea of really having ideas that come from your familiarity with natural material—there's something very human about that that gets lost when you start to take everything into this very much more abstracted way of teaching and understanding things. There's a real inherent violence in abstraction, whether at a low level when you're talking about physical materials, or at a very high level when you're talking about people or societies. I think it's an important thing to try to get students to understand this idea that there are a lot of things that you can know that are very deep things, that really are enabling, and that have a great value,

and willful amnesia. The city speaks a hundred languages,

and that nobody can tell you what they are—that you have to find it out yourself. I think that these ideas of embodied learning and learning from materials—as opposed to learning from a text, or from a lecture—they're critically important things that can get lost in the way that we teach in the modern university. But I think it's important not to lose them.

TOM JOYCE: It's also about proximity, too, isn't it? I mean, to create that uncloistered environment where the cross-disciplinary aspect is accessible—and easily. I was thinking about the Segal Design Institute at Northwestern in Chicago where Julio Ottino, the dean of the school, has opened up the center of the new building so that, no matter what your discipline was, you had an atrium-like atmosphere where you could see into the multiple floors. You could see into any of the laboratories, and you could acknowledge all the other activity that was going on. And the invitation to communicate with these other aspects—whether it's machining, or 3D printing, or robotics research—there was that. At Stanford, are the studios on campus as well, so the proximity is palpable?

HIDEO MABUCHI: I would say that we're a little bit limited by infrastructure, but not a lot. It's much more the case that students are limited by the permission they're willing to give themselves to do things that are not coding classes, or things like that. I think it's about providing good role models and structuring their educational requirements so that they're almost forced to do this—or so they can tell their parents that they had to do this.

TOM JOYCE: Whenever I take on new students, I always have them do research in what's been left behind—I mean, what our teachers have left in whatever medium. I have a library of objects and I consider them as a library, even though they're not printed material, because to be able to discern all kinds

it straddles three rivers, it holds forty islands hostage,

of subtleties about a made object, you have to turn it over and handle it, physically, with your hands. Being able to determine whether a designer was very facile at creating new ideas, or was it made for longevity, or was it an attendant maker of something else. And you can tell all these things by dissecting the different languages that are evident when one looks at the material remains of others. But along with that, looking at these other objects, I felt it was really key for students to have an understanding of making the tools, so that whatever research they wanted to investigate, they could visualize the tool that would fit their hand, their body, and be able to make whatever it was that came to mind. When I had an apprenticeship program going in the studio, I didn't really care whether the person was there to become a machinist, a welder, or an artist. It didn't matter. They had to be able to make a usable hammer, and that hammer became emblematic of the creative process that would allow many other doors to open once they had the practical understanding of that kind of facility. Yeah, then the research door is wide open. You have no limitations inside that world of making.

it is an archipelago of memory, essential and insubstantial
and evasive as the progeny of steam grates at dawn,
a gathering of apparitions. The Irish have vanished
from Washington Heights but I still see myself eating
a cold pot-roast sandwich, watching "McHale's Navy"
on a black-and-white TV in my grandmother's old apartment.
I remember the parties we used to throw on Jane Street,
shots of tequila and De La Soul on the tape deck, everyone
dancing, everyone young and vibrant and vivacious—
decades later we discovered a forgotten videotape

IX

PETER N. MILLER: Can anyone do research? I mean, is research, as you're thinking about it, something that anybody in the right circumstances or with the right prodding could do? And I'm thinking each of you can answer that in the way that you want to, but Tom, I'm thinking of the exhibition you just curated in Washington on African blacksmithing. When you think about the work that was done by the blacksmiths, do you think of the preparatory work that must have been done over whatever length of time it took to get the techniques and materials to the level of knowledge where they can produce that kind of stuff? Do you think of that as research, as research processes?

TOM JOYCE: The research among the African smiths who were developing these technologies? Absolutely. I mean, trial and error is the research component that drives whatever that activity is. In Africa, there was a very different understanding, historically, because iron was actually being produced independently of European influence or Asian influence. And so the research is evident because of the differences that were the path to success in making some of the highest quality iron available anywhere in the world. It was a different process of making in Africa than it was among the Hittites in Anatolia, or among Europeans that were figuring it out. And African smiths figured out things much earlier than European smiths did. Like, preheated air, for instance. There was a bellows design that, if you look at it from the ground in a blacksmith's shop in Africa, you would think that it looks a little bit backwards. But in fact, it couldn't be more the opposite. That was the technological innovation and the excellence with which they understood how to be able to save fuel, save time, and get the job done more quickly. You had to preheat the air so the bellows let the air just shimmy down the tube, mixing warm air from the fire, cool air inside the

and our sons, watching with bemused alarm, blurted out,

Kabre blacksmith, Kossi Kao refines the concave halves of an initiation instrument (ekpande) performed by Kabre boys undergoing a ten-year passage to manhood through phased initiation rituals. Copyright © Tom Joyce, Tcharé, 2010.

chamber, and then delivering 500°C or more air to the center of the fire. I don't know if I should keep going, but what just occurred to me is that the difference there is, that because it was small groups of related individuals making the iron, they didn't have the workforce that Europeans did, who enslaved people in different ways to have this unlimited labor source. And if you're doing the work yourself, then you figure out what it is that can save labor and be ergonomically more appropriate as a tool to use, rather than just taking something off the shelf. One good example of this is that when Europeans brought anvils—French and English and German pattern anvils and hammers—to African smiths, they tried them, and then they put them away because the tool designs that had been developed over 2,500 years were so much more efficient and ergonomically comfortable that it really put the European tools to shame. It doesn't happen abstractly.

PETER N. MILLER: So, if research is something that anyone can do—and I saw the heads nodding—is research also something that is done better in a community, or is it done better by isolated individuals? Is research a social function?

SHEILA NIRENBERG: I mean, I don't know, it depends really what research you're doing, you know? I'm sorry, I don't have a good answer for that one.

Mom, you were so beautiful! *She was. We all were,*

TOM JOYCE: It has to do with competition, too. Because the more collaborative trust that enters the equation...

SHEILA NIRENBERG: That's true.

TOM JOYCE: Yeah. And I would think that in the scientific community, there would be much more, "Eyes on the prize, but we'll keep it in a cloistered environment." Is that a really terrible assumption on my part?

SHEILA NIRENBERG: No, it's sometimes true. But I would call it more "team spirit," where we're all working on this together and the stakes are high. But I don't know if that's even about research, it's just getting the job done, in a way.

*everyone except the city. The city was a wreck and then
it was a renovation project and now it is a playground of privilege
and soon it will be something else, liquid as a dream.
Empires come and go, ours will fade in turn, even the city
will retreat, step by step, as the Atlantic rises against it.
But water is not the end. Bricks are made of clay and sand
and when they disintegrate, when they return to silt,
new bricks will be made by hands as competent as ours.
People will live in half-flooded tenements, people will live
on houseboats moored to bank pillars along Wall Street.*

X.

PETER N. MILLER: I think this is my final question. To go back
to the very beginning, where did you learn how to do this?
Do you remember the first time that you did the thing that
you now would describe as research?

MARINA RUSTOW: So, there is a pre-history and a real history.
First, the pre-history. Weirdly enough, I had to write a senior
thesis in high school, and for some reason—and I don't
know how it came to this—I wrote it on F. Scott Fitzgerald's
manuscript of *The Great Gatsby*. Which, it turns out, is
actually in the Princeton University Library where I now teach,
but which I didn't know until recently, or maybe I knew it
back then and forgot. So, there was something about this process of reading manuscripts and understanding the relationship between the kind of mind, the human hand, and the text.
I guess that's always fascinated me. When I was in college,
I had a friend who knew how to do letterpress typography
because his father was an artist and a printer. He taught me how
to do it. And again, that process of rendering things into
print, or from manuscript into print, seems always to have
fascinated me on a material level. It's not exactly research, my
answer, but there's something in this experience of exploration which is my understanding of research.

But in terms of actually sitting in front of these
Judeo-Arabic texts and figuring how to decipher them, the
way I was trained was you throw yourself into the deep-end.
You sit and you confront the manuscript, and you try to read
it with your own brain. If you look at a printed version of
it, you're cheating. That's not at all how I teach my students.
The way I teach my students is, go from the known to the
unknown. Find as many printed editions of manuscripts as you
can, compare the manuscripts with the printed edition, and
then you can take the training wheels off, which I think is a
more kind of realistic assessment. But in my generation we

It's all going under, the entire Eastern Seaboard.

were made to feel a lot of guilt about "cheating" with the printed text, which I now find to be confusing. Like, I don't know why anyone would want to live that way.

PETER N. MILLER: Terry, do you remember your first encounter with research?

TERRY PLANK: I think I hold the record for being the youngest member of the Delaware Mineralogical Society. I was eight years old, maybe seven. I grew up in a rock quarry in Wilmington, Delaware, and I studied the rocks in Delaware since I was eight. I had a microscope in my bedroom. My parents are both chemists, and like everyone in Delaware, they work for DuPont. I went to college, to Dartmouth College, to do geology. So, I just never veered, you know? I've always been fascinated with looking at the Earth, and bringing it home, and sticking it in front of a microscope—just that my microscopes have gotten fancier. The work I actually do is chemistry, so it's kind of bringing geochemical tools that are fantastic, finding colleagues who can make measurements, going to the best labs, developing some in-house, and making measurements that people haven't seen before.

PETER N. MILLER: An-My, your first encounter with research?

AN-MY LÊ: I guess, in terms of my photography, I would say trying to get access is probably the majority of the research I do. And I think, also, assessing whether something has the potential of being photographic, and giving me the results I'm looking for. But in terms of getting access, I think I learned very slowly. I think I wanted to photograph at 29 Palms, which is that Marine Corps base that's outside of LA. And I had a friend who was in the military who was a ranger in Vietnam. He taught military history, and he worked as a

The capital will move to Kansas City but nobody will mourn

for Washington. Someone will invent virtual gasoline. Someone

Events Ashore: American Sailors Returning to Vietnam, First U.S. Naval Exchange activities with Vietnam People's Navy, Da Nang, Vietnam, 2009. Copyright © An-My Lê. Courtesy of the Artist and Marian Goodman Gallery, New York, Paris, and London.

will write a poem called "At the Ruins of Yankee Stadium"

military attaché in the American embassy in Vietnam. He told me to find the public affairs department phone number and call them. And I said, "Really?" And he said, "Yes." And so I called them, and I just explained, "I'm a landscape photographer, and I'm interested in photographing military endeavors." You know, very key words. And they said, "OK, write us a letter." And I wrote the letter and repeated the same thing, and they invited me to come. And it's something that I've tried to do over and over again. It's finding the right balance in explaining what you're trying to do without giving too much information. Also, you tell them that you will show the work, and that it's a way for other people to know more about the base, to know more about the ship, or whatever. Yes, it's still frustrating because I never know whether it works or not, but somehow people think that I have the magic wand for getting access.

PETER N. MILLER: If only research had a magic wand...

TERRY PLANK: I want to know how you got access to a submarine.

AN-MY LÊ: Oh, that was a really interesting story. I never thought I could. A nuclear submarine going near the Arctic? That was my big dream, and I immediately gave up on it. Instead, I went on a Coast Guard icebreaker. In a long maritime project, I worked with the Navy, traveling all over the world. It started out as a very small thing. I wanted to photograph some Navy ships at sea, period. And the more I traveled with them, the more I found out about everything they did, the way they support science, the good things, and the blunders, and Guantanamo Bay, and everything. It turned into a nine-year project. I think I went through three public affairs officers in New York. They have three-year stints, and I was on my second public affairs officer, and they called me one day and they said, "What are you doing? Are you still working on your book?"

which will be set to a popular tune by a media impresario

They must have thought I was a crazy person who just liked to spend money and travel with the Navy. So I said, "Well, actually I have a show in New York right now. Would you like to come and see it?" I had always avoided inviting them because I was afraid they would see something that might tick them off, and then they would cut off my access forever. But this time I invited them. I had a friend who was a photography curator at MoMA, and I asked her to come for support. And so two people from the public affairs office came, and my friend Susan was there. And we kind of talked them through the pictures, and then Susan said, "Well, would you like to come and have lunch with me at MoMA next week?" And they agreed, and they came, you know, in dress whites and everything. And I think they must have been so impressed that the following week they emailed me and said, "By the way we are testing some submarines up in the Arctic. Would you like to come overnight?"

TERRY PLANK: Yes, yes!

AN-MY LÊ: But, anyway, it's a long story.

TERRY PLANK: Persistence.

TOM JOYCE: Hmm. Well, I never finished high school, so as a result, the world was wide open in terms of what kind of investigation could be extracted from any place. The town that I grew up in, El Rito, had remarkable characters everywhere you turned, each one with a kind of specialty that allowed people to put their trust in sharing whatever that information was, whether they were a farmer, or somebody who was teaching you how to make pozole and beans, or going up to the forest and peeling *latillas* [infill spanning between vigas, often small diameter peeled branches] and *vigas* [roughhewn timber tradi-

and people in Ohio will sing it during the seventh-inning stretch

tionally used as a rafter in adobe buildings] to be able to make a house, to working with mud to make an adobe. All of those aspects were informative. I think, in large measure, it created a trajectory of curiosity that would just drive in any different direction. But there was a distillation at a certain point, where that information was found to be useful, and in many different ways.

SHEILA NIRENBERG: I don't know. It was my personality as a kid to try to figure things out. I would say it that way. Back then, I wanted to be a writer. But I needed to know the answer, so I went from literature to psychology, and then I felt like that wasn't rigorous enough, and I needed to keep going. I went to neuroscience, and that wasn't rigorous enough for what I wanted to know, so then I went to math. It took a while. I was already in my 20s by then, you know. I started graduate school late—I mean, not super late, but later than other people.

I do want to say one thing, though, about the way science is. I don't know how many of you out there are also scientists, but it's not the way you think it is. And this whole idea of writing the paper and back-filling it has made a lot of people leave. Because you can't just make real discoveries or anything like that, and so a lot of people who are different and innovative have become—have left for one reason or another. [To Hideo] You've branched out. I started a company to have the freedom to do it the way that makes sense. But it's dangerous, too, because you don't want to answer to the market either. But I'm in blindness; it's just answering to an unmet need that has to be answered. But if you're being peer reviewed by people who are pedantic or whatever—pedestrian in their thinking is really the right word—it forces your grants to be that way. At some point you just might say, "Screw it. I'm just going to raise money and try to do the thing that couldn't get a grant—something that has meaning, that answers that question of purpose, or can satisfy something either in me or can make the world better." And it's too bad that science is

remembering, or imagining, the glory of what was.

like this. I don't know how it happens, but it evolves that way. Am I capturing your—

HIDEO MABUCHI: Yes, yes, yes. I agree with you a 100%. And the unfortunate thing is that science is really expensive. [*laughing*]

SHEILA NIRENBERG: And so, I was going to say, in his case, because it's physics, so many papers have 400 authors and giant, giant, giant pieces of equipment, and I'm not exaggerating, right?

HIDEO MABUCHI: No. This is definitely true in parts of physics. Not in my part of physics, but yes.

SHEILA NIRENBERG: OK. But I can still publish a two author paper, and our field is still a little calmer, and the equipment I need is not so big, so it's a little bit less... political, in a way. Because you have to know the right person who has access to the right machine, or you can't do the experiment in physics— there are a lot of things that are like that.

PETER N. MILLER: You mentioned machines. Can machines do research?

MARINA RUSTOW: Can I jump into that? Artificial intelligence has completely revolutionized my work in ways that I could not possibly have foreseen when I started out, and in two different ways. One has already happened, and is amazing, which is that computer vision has made it possible to piece fragments— disjointed fragments of manuscripts—together again. It's not always a successful process, but it's been fascinating to watch.

Time is with us viscerally, idiomatically, time inhabits us

And it's definitely sped up what we do, which is to say it's much nicer to be able to read the whole letter than just half of it. These algorithms were put online in about 2012, and the first time I ever tried it, I plugged in a document from the 15th century that I'd been working with that was only a top half. And, well, how did I know it was 15th century? I didn't; I was just guessing based on the paleography. And the very first time I used the algorithm, I got the bottom half, which had the date on it, and it was 1463. I remember thinking, "I can't believe this just happened." The software's not always right, but it's made a lot of progress.

The second way is happening right now, and so I don't know what's going to happen with it. Handwritten text recognition, which is essentially like OCR (Optical Character Recognition), but for manuscript texts. I was very skeptical at first. What you're doing is you're training a computer to be able to read handwriting that sometimes you, as a human being, can't read. And even if you can read it, you know, there is a lot of work to be done. The idea is that you plug in a certain amount of information you're certain of—let's say, 500 letters written in Hebrew script in the 11th century—and you can then actually get the machine to learn to read other letters from the 11th century.

There are different teams working on this in Hebrew, and Arabic, and Syriac, and Latin in different places in the world. At first, it made me nervous because I was like, "Are we going to not teach our students paleography?" I mean they have to know how to decipher! And then I realized that it's actually a completely complimentary process—that you can have the computer do certain things, and then that leads you to a deeper understanding of what you are doing with your human eye. So, that's just starting out and it's very exciting.

TERRY PLANK: You're much further along. We're still working on this. Built into our volcano array is a machine learning algorithm aspect. The signals of the run-up to an eruption, what do those look like? And is looking at patterns useful?

like a glass bowl filled with tap water at the kitchen sink,

But we're not there yet. We still haven't collected the data in many cases.

AN-MY LÊ: I use the extremely old and the extremely new together. I still carry a 5×7 large format view camera that I use to shoot film. I have to load the film and put it in the dark box, but I scan the film and output it using Photoshop. I mean, there are some incredibly great digital cameras that are so sharp and have huge files, but I feel that at least at this point, the size of my negative is still providing a kind of physical experience— a three-dimensionality to my prints—that the digital camera can't. I mean, it would make things look sharper than some of my things, but it doesn't give you the sense that things are not stacked against each other, that there is air flowing between objects that are behind one another. And so I still use film. But I use Photoshop a lot.

HIDEO MABUCHI: Before we go, I want to say one more thing about research. That rather than it being a thing about science specifically, I think the issue in all of this is the professionalization of your passions. That's a really difficult thing to navigate. One thing that I'll say in favor of academia is: in ten years, you can get yourself a stable job on the basis of the scientific work that you've done, and then turn to other things that you might want to do, that are teaching initiatives or whatever, that are pretty much free to do. And that's a great situation to be in.

In the physical sciences, we do a very good job, I think, of trying to teach rigor. As to this kind of two-part thing that you introduced before, I think we do a terrible job of teaching students how to be creative and pick good topics. I always think back to when I was in college. Any of the math or physics courses that I took, the way that we were assigned homework is, every week they give you a list of problems that are related to the material of the week, and you had to solve those problems. So, sort of, like, somebody gives you

and some little pink stones, and a sunken plastic castle

the problems and you solve them. Whereas in, say, literature classes or philosophy classes, it's more like, "Here's a book. Tell me something interesting about this book." But it's actually that latter kind of thing that, in the end, is much more important for making you a good researcher. Because, you know, being good or being impactful as a researcher is much more about asking the right questions—things that other people haven't thought to ask, things that really kind of cut into some crucial sort of issue. So, I would say that's a very important skill that we don't do a very good job of teaching, but somehow it gets to the core of what it really means to be good at doing research.

with a child's face etched in a slate-grey window.
Fish swim past, solemn as ghosts, and the child smiles sadly,
wondering, perhaps, how bees will pollinate underwater.
He seems a little melancholy. He must miss his old home,
a skin-honeyed hive of multifarious humankind,
a metropolis of stately filth doused in overrich perfume.
The castle door swings open and the boy emerges
like an astronaut stepping warily onto the moon.
When he sees us, through the warping lens of the bowl,
watching him with desperate, misfocused passion, we are
as cartoonishly gargantuan as the past, and he as spectral

Courtesy of Jackson McGrath. *Waterfront*, Haverstraw, NY. Digital photograph.

as the future, raising one small hand to wave goodbye.

ANNIE DORSEN is a theatre director and writer producing works that dramatize the complex interface between machines and humans. Dorsen creates what she calls "algorithmic theatre," in which algorithmically-determined texts are generated in real time for each performance of a piece. Dorsen has shifted her focus to the nature of social interaction in the digital world in recent pieces such as *The Great Outdoors* (2017), in which the incalculable corpus of the internet is juxtaposed with the vastness of our universe. Audience members lie in an inflatable planetarium and watch a display of stars overhead while a performer reads text—sometimes banal, sometimes deeply personal—scraped from chatrooms, comment threads, and message boards across the internet. Dorsen's investigations of the creative possibilities engendered by the rise of artificial intelligence are challenging the definition of a theatrical event while also encouraging audiences to contemplate the ways in which nonhuman intelligence is profoundly changing the nature of work, culture, and social relationships. Annie received her BA (1996) and an MFA (2000) from Yale University. Her additional works include *Infinite Sun* (2019), *The Slow Room* (2018), and *Spokaoke* (2012), and she was the co-creator and director of *Passing Strange* (2008). Her work has been performed at such national and international venues as Performance Space New York (formerly PS 122), the Brooklyn Academy of Music, On the Boards, the Museum of Contemporary Art, Chicago, the National Theatre of Scotland, and Théâtre de la Cité in Paris, among others. Since 2017, Dorsen has served as a visiting assistant professor of practice with the Committee on Theatre and Performance Studies at the University of Chicago.

ELODIE GHEDIN is a biomedical researcher who is harnessing the power of genomic sequencing techniques to generate critical insights about human pathogens. Although the technology for obtaining nucleotide sequence data continues to accelerate, the labor-intensive task of analyzing and annotating the resulting data—for example, identifying genes, their functions, and their expression; determining the arrangement of genes within the genome; performing phylogenetic and functional comparisons with other known species—often lags behind. Ghedin has established herself as a leader of international projects that coordinate the efforts of scores of scientists to decode the function of some of the most virulent human pathogens. A major focus of her work has been parasites that cause diseases endemic to tropical climates, such as leishmaniasis, sleeping sickness, Chagas disease, elephantiasis, and river blindness. Through her direct research and mobilization of global scientific collaborations, Ghedin's work illuminates the similarities and differences in the molecular physiology of the various parasites, with important implications for targets for drug development. In addition, Ghedin and her colleagues are applying similar approaches to understanding viruses that infect humans. RNA viruses such as HIV and influenzae mutate particularly rapidly, making vaccine development difficult. In a high-resolution study of complete genome sequences of influenza A from thousands of isolates collected in the New York area, Ghedin and colleagues showed that the virus evolves with surprising rapidity even in a circumscribed geographic region. Through her contributions to parasitology and virology, Ghedin demonstrates that molecular genetics is not only essential for exploring the basic biology of pathogens but also represents a powerful tool in the hands of scientists working in coordination to improve public health across the globe.

TOM JOYCE is a sculptor and widely acknowledged as one of the foremost practitioners in the field for his contributions to the art and science of forging iron. Initially trained as a blacksmith in the rural farming community of El Rito, New Mexico in his youth, Joyce's works examine the physical, environmental, political, and historical implications of using iron as a primary medium. Working from studios in Santa Fe,

New Mexico; Brussels, Belgium; and at several industrial forging and foundry facilities in the US, his concerns and observations are expressed through multimedia installations, immersive soundscapes, video projections, photography, and through materials that have inherited specific histories from prior use.

HIDEO MABUCHI is a physicist who uses optical methods to extend our understanding of quantum behavior. Mabuchi's studies provide an experimental vehicle for exploring how thermodynamic processes mask quantum behavior, and how their interaction might be harnessed for important practical uses. Using optical trapping protocols, he investigates the effects of external perturbations on quantum behavior. Mabuchi specifically focuses on examining the long-term dynamic evolution of quantum systems. This line of research is establishing the groundwork for future advances in both fundamental physics and practical applications. In addition, physics at the intersection of the quantum and thermodynamic regimes may play a vital role in determining the conformation of large biomolecules (such as enzymes) whose function depends on correct three-dimensional structure. Mabuchi received his AB in physics from Princeton University (1992) and PhD in physics from California Institute of Technology (1998). He spent nine years as a faculty member at Caltech with appointments in physics and in control and dynamical systems, then moved to Stanford University as professor of applied physics in 2007. He has been serving as chair of the Applied Physics Department since September 2010. Selected honors include an A.P. Sloan Foundation Research Fellowship, an Office of Naval Research Young Investigator Award, and the inaugural Mohammed Dahleh Distinguished Lectureship awarded by University of California, Santa Barbara.

CAMPBELL MCGRATH is a poet whose work is characterized by lyrical skill, intellectual breadth, and humor. McGrath's most recent books are *Nouns & Verbs: New and Selected Poems* (Ecco Press, 2019), and *XX: Poems for the Twentieth Century*, a finalist for the 2016 Pulitzer Prize. In it, as in his other work, he combines both a personal and an acute historical consciousness as he maps the social, cultural, and natural landscapes of America. His grand vision, raw energy, and keen ear for the subtleties of the modern condition have led critics to compare him to Allen Ginsberg and William Carlos Williams. Though his work is a reflection of our age and society, McGrath has his own unique voice—an expansive prose poetry that accumulates images and metaphors through the use of symbols and tangible, everyday details. McGrath is the Philip and Patricia Frost Professor of Creative Writing and a professor of English at Florida International University. He is the author of *Capitalism* (1990), *American Noise* (1994), *Spring Comes to Chicago* (1996), *Road Atlas* (2001), *Florida Poems* (2002), and *Pax Atomica* (2004). His work has been published in such literary magazines as the *Paris Review* and the *Kenyon Review*. McGrath received a BA (1984) from the University of Chicago and an MFA (1988) from Columbia University.

PETER N. MILLER, dean of Bard Graduate Center, works in the history of historical research. Miller is interested in questions historians ask, or even more precisely, how historians turn "survivals" into evidence. His thinking has been spurred by a long-running engagement with early modern European antiquarianism and its continuing impact on how historians work. Selected recent publications include *History and its Objects: Antiquarianism and Material Culture Since 1500* (Cornell University Press, 2017) and *Peiresc's Mediterranean World* (Cambridge: Harvard University Press, 2015). He is also an editor of BGC's book series *Cultural Histories of the Material World* published by the University of Michigan Press. Miller holds a PhD from the University of Cambridge, and a BA and MA from Harvard University.

AN-MY LÊ was born in Saigon, Vietnam, in 1960. Lê fled Vietnam with her family as a teenager in 1975, the final year of the war, eventually settling in the United States as a political refugee. Lê received BAS and MS degrees in biology from Stanford University (1981, 1985) and an MFA from Yale University (1993). Her photographs and films examine the impact, consequences, and representation of war. Whether in color or black and white, her pictures frame a tension between the natural landscape and its violent transformation into battlefields. Projects include *Viêt Nam* (1994–98), in which Lê's memories of a war-torn countryside are reconciled with the contemporary landscape; *Small Wars* (1999–2002), in which Lê photographed and participated in Vietnam War reenactments in South Carolina; and *29 Palms* (2003–04), in which US Marines preparing for deployment play-act scenarios in a virtual Middle East in the California desert. Suspended between the formal traditions of documentary and staged photography, Lê's work explores the disjunction between wars as historical events and the ubiquitous representation of war in contemporary entertainment, politics, and collective consciousness.

SHEILA NIRENBERG is a neuroscientist exploring fundamental questions about how the brain encodes visual information and developing an alternative approach to restoring sight after photoreceptor cell degeneration. In the visual sensory system in mammals, the photoreceptor cells in the retina take in information from the outside world, such as an image or visual pattern. This information is then passed through the retinal circuitry to the ganglion cells, which transform it into a neural code that the brain can understand. In the case of diseases such as macular degeneration and retinitis pigmentosa, which affect approximately 20–25 million people worldwide, vision is lost when deteriorating photoreceptor cells no longer take in visual signals.

TERRY PLANK is a geochemist working literally at the edge of phenomena shaping the Earth's crust. Her research focuses on what happens when tectonic plates collide, forcing one under the other at a subduction zone. Because these collisions generate tremendous heat, they are frequently associated with volcanoes, which Plank uses as a window to the chemical and physical forces deep below the surface. In early work, she analyzed trace metals in deep core samples from rock entering a subduction zone and compared them with magma ejected from associated volcanoes, finding that the magma unexpectedly includes materials from the subducted crust, rather than exclusively new rock formed from the Earth's mantle. More recently, she has demonstrated that the chemical composition of volcanic rocks reveals the temperature at the point of rock formation, where the subduction plate intersects the mantle. These data are essential for accurate modeling of tectonic geophysics. Furthermore, her observations of certain volcanic minerals that trap water demonstrate the critical role they play in the geochemistry of rock formation at subduction zones (it is water and other volatiles that account for the volcanic explosions). Though the motion of tectonic plates triggers some of the Earth's greatest spectacles—earthquakes, pyroclastic lava flows, geysers, etc.—the science of plate tectonics is still in its early stages. With painstaking fieldwork, careful analysis, and profound insight, Plank is uncovering details about the complex interplay of thermal and chemical forces that drives this usually imperceptible but remarkably powerful natural force.

MARINA RUSTOW is a historian using the Cairo Geniza texts to shed new light on Jewish life and on the broader society of the medieval Middle East. The Cairo Geniza (or Genizah) comprises hundreds of thousands of legal documents, letters, and literary materials—many of them fragmentary—deposited in Cairo's Ben Ezra Synagogue over more than a millennium. Rustow's approach to this archive goes beyond decoding documents, in itself a formidable task, to questioning the relationship between subjects and medieval states and asking what that relationship tells us about power and the negotiation of religious boundaries. Rustow's current work addresses Geniza documents in Arabic script from the Fatimid caliphate. Using a bidirectional lens—that is, interpreting the material from the point of view of both the Islamic and Jewish communities—Rustow is mining these documents for what they can tell us about how the caliphal state ruled and how Jewish, Christian, and Muslim subjects related to it.

Campbell McGrath
At the Ruins of Yankee Stadium

It is that week in April when all the lions start to shine,
café tables poised for selfies, windows squeegeed
and fenceposts freshly painted around Tompkins Square,
former haven of junkies and disgraceful pigeons
today chock-full of French bulldogs and ornamental tulips
superimposed atop the old, familiar, unevictable dirt.
Lying on the couch, I am drifting with the conversation
of bees, a guttural buzz undergirding the sound
from a rusty string of wind chimes hung and forgotten
in the overgrown beech tree marooned out back,
limbs shaggy with neon-green flame-tongue leaflets
forking through a blanket of white blossoms,
long-neglected evidence of spring at its most deluxe,
pure exuberant fruitfulness run amok.
Rigorous investigation has identified two dialects
buzzing through the plunder-fall, hovering black bumblebees
and overworked honeybees neck deep in nectar-bliss,
as the city to us, blundering against its oversaturated anthers
until the pollen coats our skin, as if sugar-dusted,
as if rolled in honey and flour to bake a cake
for the queen, yes, she is with us, it is spring and this
is her coronation, blossoming pear and crab-apple
and cherry trees, too many pinks to properly absorb,
every inch of every branch lusting after beauty.
To this riot of stimuli, this vernal bombardment
of the senses, I have capitulated without a fight.
But not the beech tree. It never falters. It is stalwart
and grounded and garlanded, a site-specific creation,
seed to rootling to this companionable giant,
tolerant and benign, how many times have I reflected
upon their superiority to our species, the trees of earth?
Reflection, self-reflection—my job is to polish the mirror,
to amplify the echoes. Even now I am hard at work,
researching the ineffable. *I loafe and invite my soul*,
for Walt Whitman is ever my companion in New York,
thronged carcass of a city in which one is never alone
and yet never un-nagged-at by loneliness, a hunger
as much for the otherness of others as for the much-sung self,
for something somewhere on the verge of realization,
for what lies around the corner, five or six blocks uptown,
hiding out in the Bronx or across the river in Jersey.

Somewhere on the streets of the city right now somebody
is meeting the love of their life for the very first time,
somebody is drinking schnapps from a paper sack
discussing Monty Python with a man impersonating a priest,
someone is waiting for the bus to South Carolina
to visit her sister in hospice, someone is teleconferencing
with the office back in Hartford, Antwerp, Osaka,
someone is dust-sweeping, throat-clearing, cartwheeling,
knife-grinding, day-trading, paying dues, dropping a dime,
giving the hairy eyeball, pissing against a wall,
someone is snoozing, sniffling, cavorting, nibbling,
roistering, chiding, snuggling, confiding,
pub-crawling, speed-dating, pump-shining, ivy-trimming,
tap-dancing, curb-kicking, rat-catching, tale-telling,
getting lost, getting high, getting busted, breaking up,
breaking down, breaking loose, losing faith,
going broke, going green, feeling blue, seeing red,
someone is davening, busking, hobnobbing, grandstanding,
playing the ponies, feeding the pigeons, gull-watching,
wolf-whistling, badgering the witness, pulling down the grill
and locking up shop, writing a letter home in Pashto or
Xhosa, learning to play the xylophone, waiting for an Uber X,
conspiring, patrolling, transcending, bedeviling,
testifying, bloviating, absolving, kibitzing,
kowtowing, pinky-swearing, tarring and shingling,
breaking and entering, delivering and carting away,
enwreathing lampposts with yellow ribbons,
reading Apollinaire on a bench littered with fallen petals,
waiting for an ambulance to pass before crossing First Avenue
toward home. No wonder they fear it so intensely,
the ideologues and isolationists in Kansas and Kandahar, it is a
relentless negotiation with multiplicity,
a constant engagement with the shape-shifting mob,
diversely luminous as sunlight reflecting off mirrored glass
in puzzle pieces of apostolic light. Certainly this is not
the Eternal City but it is certainly Imperial, certainly
tyrannical, democratic, demagogic, dynastic, anarchic,
hypertrophic, hyperreal. An empire of rags and photons.
An empire encoded in the bricks from which it was built,
each a stamped emblem of its labor-intensive materiality,
hundreds of millions barged down the Hudson each year
from the clay pits of Haverstraw and Kingston
after the Great Fire of 1835, a hinterland of dependencies,
quarries and factories and arterial truck farms
delivering serum to that muscular heart, a toiling collective

of Irish sandhogs and Iroquois beam walkers and Ivoirian
umbrella vendors collecting kindling for the bonfire
that has lured, like moths, the entire world to its blaze.
As with my tree, the hubbub of bees its exaltation.
Apis, maker of honey, *Bombus*, the humble bumbler,
and the tree a common American beech.
It rules the yard, overawing a straggling ailanthus
hard against the wall of the Con Ed substation.
Along the fence some scraggly boxwood shrubs,
a table collapsed into rusted segments, two piles of bricks—
what's their story?—who made them, carted them,
set them as a patio, and who undid that work to create these
mundane, rain-eroded monuments to human neglect?
Why does nobody tend this little garden?
Undisciplined ivy scales the building in thick ropes
and coils of porcelain berry vine, whose fruit will ripen
to obscene brilliance come autumn, those strange berries,
turquoise, violet, azure... Ah, I've lost my train
of thought. Berries. The city. People, bricks, the past.
Bees in a flowering beech tree. Symbiosis. Streams and webs
and permutations, viruses replicating, mutating, evolving.
Books in a library, bricks in a wall, people in a city.
A man selling old golf clubs on the corner of Ludlow Street.
A woman on the F train carefully rubbing ointment
up and down her red, swollen arms. Acorns—
tossing them into the Hudson River from a bench as I did
when I was Peter Stuyvesant, when I was Walt Whitman,
when we were of the Lenape and Broadway our hunting trail.
Then the deer vanished, the docks decayed, the towers fell.
The African graveyard was buried beneath concrete
as the memory of slavery has been obscured by metonymy
and willful amnesia. The city speaks a hundred languages,
it straddles three rivers, it holds forty islands hostage,
it is an archipelago of memory, essential and insubstantial
and evasive as the progeny of steam grates at dawn,
a gathering of apparitions. The Irish have vanished
from Washington Heights but I still see myself eating
a cold pot-roast sandwich, watching "McHale's Navy"
on a black-and-white TV in my grandmother's old apartment.
I remember the parties we used to throw on Jane Street,
shots of tequila and De La Soul on the tape deck, everyone
dancing, everyone young and vibrant and vivacious—
decades later we discovered a forgotten videotape
and our sons, watching with bemused alarm, blurted out,
Mom, you were so beautiful! She was. We all were,

everyone except the city. The city was a wreck and then
it was a renovation project and now it is a playground of privilege
and soon it will be something else, liquid as a dream.
Empires come and go, ours will fade in turn, even the city
will retreat, step by step, as the Atlantic rises against it.
But water is not the end. Bricks are made of clay and sand
and when they disintegrate, when they return to silt,
new bricks will be made by hands as competent as ours.
People will live in half-flooded tenements, people will live
on houseboats moored to bank pillars along Wall Street.
It's all going under, the entire Eastern Seaboard.
The capital will move to Kansas City but nobody will mourn
for Washington. Someone will invent virtual gasoline. Someone
will write a poem called "At the Ruins of Yankee Stadium"
which will be set to a popular tune by a media impresario
and people in Ohio will sing it during the seventh-inning stretch
remembering, or imagining, the glory of what was.
Time is with us viscerally, idiomatically, time inhabits us
like a glass bowl filled with tap water at the kitchen sink,
and some little pink stones, and a sunken plastic castle
with a child's face etched in a slate-grey window.
Fish swim past, solemn as ghosts, and the child smiles sadly,
wondering, perhaps, how bees will pollinate underwater.
He seems a little melancholy. He must miss his old home,
a skin-honeyed hive of multifarious humankind,
a metropolis of stately filth doused in overrich perfume.
The castle door swings open and the boy emerges
like an astronaut stepping warily onto the moon.
When he sees us, through the warping lens of the bowl,
watching him with desperate, misfocused passion, we are
as cartoonishly gargantuan as the past, and he as spectral
as the future, raising one small hand to wave goodbye.